American Nymph Fly-Fishing Guide

River Trout, Stillwater Species, and Steelhead

Michael Gorman

American Nymph Fly-Fishing Guide

River Trout, Stillwater Species, and Steelhead

Michael Gorman

Frank Amato
Publications

Dedication

I am a fortunate man to have a brother who is a good man, a loyal friend, and a skilled fly-fishing partner. Together we are Batman and Robin, Butch and the Sundance Kid, and, sometimes, Laurel & Hardy. Patrick Gorman is the embodiment of all that is good about the fly-fishing experience—a thoughtful practitioner, respecter of the fish and all that surrounds them, and a conversational and witty companion. In short, he is the best brother a fly-fisher ever had.

All inquiries should be addressed to:
Frank Amato Publications, Inc.
P.O. Box 82112
Portland, Oregon 97282
(503) 653-8108
www.AmatoBooks.com

ISBN-13: 978-1-57188-529-6
UPC: 0-81127-00382-2
Printed in Singapore
10 9 8 7 6 5 4 3 2 1

Contents

Introduction

I have written this book for those fly-anglers interested in catching more fish on a consistent basis. Why should you listen to me? What authority and credentials do I have? I have been pursuing fish since I was in the third grade. I always wanted to catch more fish than anyone else. A mix of greed and intense pride, definitely a sinful combination for a young boy growing up Catholic. After a brief career teaching secondary school math and science I opened a fly-fishing shop, the Scarlet Ibis, in Corvallis, Oregon. Knowing how important possessing fly-fishing skills and catching fish are to the financial success of a fishing business, I set out to learn whatever was necessary to continue to be able to catch a variety of freshwater species on a fly. Lots of fish. More fish than anyone else, if I could. Then I could humbly regale my customers with my fishing stories—complete with photographs—and tell them how they could do the same with the equipment and flies to be purchased from me.

Besides being the main retail guy, I also designated myself the head fishing guide. Not only did I need to possess mad fly-fishing expertise, I had to enable my clients to catch fish with me, even those who had never held a fly rod in their hands before our day together on the water. It is one thing to possess skills, but a totally different game to be able to *effectively* teach these skills. Motivated by pride (again!) and the financial need to grow a solid business, I had to constantly refine and update my fish-catching and teaching competencies. And, I did. And, continue to do so to this day, decades later.

Though I am intimately familiar with all fly-fishing methods, including variations and derivatives of these techniques, one stands above all the others for consistent, fish-catching effectiveness for species in both moving-water environments and stillwaters.

Nymphing is hands-down my first choice of all the fly-fishing methods to catch fish. As a professional fly-fishing guide who must enable my clients to catch fish on a fly rod so they will want to fish with me again someday, and tell their friends, nymph fishing is most often the technique that will catch more fish than either wet flies or dry flies. I do use and teach all fly-fishing methods, but nymph fishing is my bread and butter, my pièce de résistance, the crown jewel, my assassin's tool, the Ultimate Down & Dirty, and my One True Love.

For a variety of reasons some anglers may not share my enthusiasm for nymph fishing. A select few may actually disdain this technique, relegating themselves to fishing only dry flies or wet flies. I am happy for them. They will offer little competition for me as I fish behind them and catch those fish which have shown little or no interest in their flies and methods.

A second group of fly-fishers may have dabbled a little with this technique, but do not fish nymphs because they have not taken the time to learn how to effectively use this method, catching only the occasional suicidal fish.

They may believe this technique too complicated or ineffective, and, thus, give up on learning successful nymphing skills.

In the credit fly-fishing classes I teach at Oregon State University I make sure to emphasize the importance of nymph fishing, and its many details. I will easily dedicate triple the classroom time to nymphing compared to angling with wet flies or dry flies, attempting to maximize the opportunities for my students' fish-catching success.

Nymphing is, in my opinion, the most involved and detail-driven of the fly-fishing methods. Maybe even mysterious to some. It is a game of details. Ignore or overlook just one of these details and no fish will be caught. As a result, an unskilled or unthinking fisherman may assume the fish are not in a biting mood, when just the opposite may be true.

The author taught credit fly-fishing classes at Oregon State University for more than 27 years.

In the pages that follow I am going to dissect the necessary elements of successful nymph fishing, and reveal what I have learned over decades of personal pursuits, and teaching my guided fly-fishing clients. These will include the specific rod/reel/fly line equipment for the particular fish species and their environments, the best leader and tippet setup, mending and line control, aquatic entomology, fly selection, detecting subtle strikes, and the proper hook-set. (Yes, not one in fifty fly-anglers set the hook effectively!) I will detail catching selected species in their particular environments: trout in streams and rivers, trout and warm-water species in lakes and ponds, and steelhead in streams and rivers. Each combination of species and environment requires specific examination of the just-mentioned necessary nymphing elements. Each combination has its unique set of challenges which will be addressed, including equipment, flies, and a strategic fishing game plan outlined for the reader.

This book will have special appeal for those thoughtful anglers who welcome and enjoy the challenges of nymphing. Fly-fishing is about successful puzzle solving. On any given day the puzzle pieces may be a little different than the day before, and the pieces will fit together a little differently, too.

Pinch me. People actually pay me to solve fly-fishing puzzles. The fishing day's typical questions: Where are the fish? What are they eating today? What fly will catch them? How should the fly be presented to fool the fish? What must be done when the strike happens? Once the fish is on the line, how do we get it to the net without losing it? And, how can we successfully get a photo without harming a fish that may be released?

If I want to continue to get paid for my puzzle-solving skills I must successfully find the solutions, enabling my guests to catch fish, and participate in making happy memories. This isn't always easy. There are many variables that come into play in successfully charming the fish every day: water, weather, insect activity, competition from other guides and anglers, successfully teaching and enabling a beginner to catch fish, and—hardest of all—re-programming a know-it-all angler who has many bad habits.

When not pursuing fish, Sudoku is my thinking game of choice. I love these puzzles, specifically difficult ones. Fly-fishing is puzzle solving in beautiful places. It calls me constantly. I think you are blessed if it calls you, too. And, fortunately for us, there will always be one more puzzle to solve. Nymphing has many of the fly-fishing puzzle answers if we are sharp enough to discover and learn them.

ONE

Nymphing: An Overview of Fly-Fishing's Deadliest Method

The ransom note reads: "If you ever want to see your cat again you must catch a fish on a fly today, and deliver it to the designated drop site tonight. Come alone. We will be watching." You can safely bet I WILL pay the ransom for my sweet Squeaky Cat. I WILL catch a fish on a fly today. And, I WILL be using the nymph fishing method to do it.

Three Choices

There are three general fly-fishing methods, which correspond to the three general categories of artificial flies: dry fly, wet fly, and nymph. A nymph fly is a reference to an artificial designed to imitate an immature aquatic insect. Generally, nymph fishing evolved as a technique whereby an imitation of an immature aquatic insect is presented under the water's surface to the fish in such a manner that it will fool the fish into believing the fly is a living creature to be eaten. Depending on the environment (moving water vs. stillwater) and the insect being imitated, there are multiple variations of the nymph fishing method.

Where Fish Spend Their Time

It makes sense that fish spend most of their time near the bottom of the stream, river, lake, or pond in which they live. Besides the possibilities of a place to hide from creatures which might eat them, a retreat from the bright light of a high sun, and the comfort of slower currents, in the case of those fish living in moving waters, there is one last very important reason that fish cruise the bottom most of their lives: that's where the food is. Among the rocks, water plants, and debris live the vast majority of aquatic organisms that fish eat. So, it only makes good sense that an angler fishes the fly near the bottom most of the time.

90% of Their Diet!

Ninety percent is a very commonly repeated number when referencing the importance of nymphs to a trout's diet. I have no reason to doubt this number. Even if it is only 66 2/3 % which nymphs contribute to the trout's menu, this still overwhelms the contribution of other food items, such as other fish, leeches, and adult insects. So, playing the odds, nymph fishing is the logical fly-fishing method of choice.

Stonefly nymphs are quite prevalent in Western rivers. Some species provide a substantial mouthful for trout and steelhead.

Nymphs often make up the vast majority of a fish's diet. Logically, use nymph imitations to catch fish.

Nymph fishing is a balancing act. The goal is to convincingly present an artificial fly so a fish will be fooled into eating it. Those factors which must be correctly married together, then, include the right fly, at the right depth, swimming or drifting the fly like the real-life foods the fish commonly sees, and detecting the strike. There can be nothing haphazard or careless in any of these elements. Each will be examined in meticulous detail in the chapters which follow.

Nymphs vs. the Nymphing Method

Taxonomically speaking, a "nymph" is an immature life stage of an aquatic insect with a three-stage life cycle. The three stages are egg, nymph, and adult.

Those aquatic insects with four life stages start out as a tiny egg, and then transition into the larva, pupa, and adult. Though they are technically not "nymphs",

flies imitating the larvae and pupae of certain insects are deadly for catching fish. These flies can be effectively fished using the nymph fishing *method*. So, successful nymphing or nymph fishing may actually involve using non-nymph fly patterns.

The same holds true for those flies that imitate salmon or steelhead eggs, which fish love to eat. These are certainly not nymphs, but the nymph fishing *method* is used to present the flies to the fish.

Not So Simple

At first glance, nymph fishing seems a simple matter. Cast a fly into the water, allow it to sink, perhaps pull on the line now and then to make it swim or twitch, set the hook, and reel in the prize. In reality, however, effective nymph fishing can be a complex matter because of all the necessary elements which go into fooling a fish and detecting the interception of the fly, which can

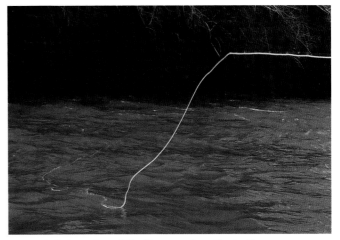

Brightly-colored fly lines and strike indicators are standard equipment for most nymph anglers.

Since they must feed on a regular basis, nymph fishing for trout is a logical starting point for those new to the technique. This brown trout ate one of my All-Star nymphs, the Bead Head Serendipity.

be subtle. Because the nymph (or non-insect fly-fished using the nymphing method, such as one imitating a salmon egg) is fished under water, out of sight, often with a slack line which allows it to sink, an angler may not get the necessary feedback to know he is fishing the nymph effectively.

Over the span of my many years of fly-fishing, teaching fly-fishing classes, and guiding, I have encountered thousands of anglers. I have met many, many anglers who have caught fish on nymphs, but a tiny handful of good nymph fishermen. Very, very few anglers who professed to be experienced nymph fishermen were effective at it. Even though some have caught countless fish, only a small handful of them would be good enough to entice selective or highly-cautious fish. Most nymphers don't understand or pay attention to necessary details that contribute to maximum effectiveness, concerning leaders, droppers, angle of presentation, weighting, and mending, subtle strike detection, and the correct hook-set.

Everyone who fishes nymphs will eventually accumulate stories about the days they had nonstop, killer fishing. Maybe a day on which they caught "a hundred fish".

Such days may trick the angler into believing he knows just about all there is to know about this method. This is a trap. The true test and the learning come on those days when the fish are not foolish and suicidal. Those days when you, and everyone around you, are not catching fish . . . except that one angler keeping to himself as he quietly reels in another fish. It's not luck; it may not be the Secret Fly, or the lucky location. His success is most likely the details of the leader, effective mending, and subtle strike detection.

The Logical Beginning

Most fly-anglers begin their nymphing efforts with fishing trout in streams and rivers. Since locating the exact positions where fish station themselves is half the success formula, stream fishing for hungry trout is the best place to start with the highest probability of nymphing success.

The Next Challenge

The next logical transition for most fly-anglers who have had some nymphing success in moving waters is to stillwaters. Many are motivated by the possibilities of more fish and bigger fish available in lakes and ponds. Quality stillwaters are, indeed, capable of producing more food per square foot over its entire area than most quality rivers. More food = more and bigger fish. Though the rewards can be bigger, the attendant challenges are bigger, especially in locating the ever-moving fish and their penchant for changing food preferences often. These are two of the primary stumbling blocks for frustrated fly-anglers who are too often humbled on lakes, then desert them and return to the easier challenges of stream nymphing.

Nymphing for the Ultimate Freshwater Prize

My most popular guiding venue is teaching clients how to catch steelhead on a fly. Anglers just love to catch big, challenging fish. In order for me to maintain and grow my guiding business I must maximize the opportunities for my guests to hook and catch steelhead.

Nymph fishing is absolutely critical to my clients' fish-catching success, winter and summer, so I have carved out my guiding niche as a nymphing specialist. Besides the matter of me wanting to catch every fish in the river myself, I have been doubly motivated to dissect, understand, and effectively execute every element of the nymph fishing method to teach and guide successfully.

When it comes to pursuing and catching steelhead, there are additional challenges. At the top of the list is the fact that there are very few steelhead per mile of river at any given time compared to the number of trout available in a quality river. This means my clients will have only a handful of opportunities in an 8-hour fishing day. I must enable them to make the most of these few opportunities. I will fish dry flies and wet flies with my clients, particularly early, before the sun is on the water. But most of a typical steelhead day will be dedicated to nymphing, which may include fishing a salmon egg imitation utilizing the nymph-fishing method. Every moment with my clients I am the coach. I call all the plays from the rower's seat. I watch every cast that is made, and I coach every detail of the cast, presentation, and hook-set. I am watching for a strike even as my guests stare at a bald eagle flying overhead or a deer swimming the river ahead of us, knowing that the strike often happens when it is least expected. All this is a good test for my nymphing skills because I am fishing every cast by proxy, fishing through my clients. Not only must I understand nymph fishing, I must be able to convey it verbally to my guests, some of whom have never nymphed in their lives.

So, if you are a rank beginner, a nymphing dabbler, or an experienced angler who has had some nymphing success, my overriding goal is to clearly detail and logically lay out the many details and nuances of this deadly method.

Steelhead are the ultimate freshwater nymphing prize. Because their appetites are temperamental, honed nymphing skills and persistence are necessary for consistent success.

With good instruction on a quality river even a first-time fly-angler like Barbara Wilson may catch a steelhead (or four) on a nymph.

TWO

Fish Foods: Aquatic Entomology

The inspirations for nymph fly patterns come from the immature aquatic insects that fish eat. To be the ultimate nymph angler, one need be familiar with aquatic entomology, at least at a cursory level.

Everyone is familiar with the life cycle of the butterfly: egg, caterpillar, chrysalis, and the adult insect. Aquatic insects pass through various life stages, too, on their way to adulthood.

In the aquatic realm, insects will have one of two life cycles: complete metamorphosis or incomplete metamorphosis, which are four stages or three stages respectively.

Complete metamorphosis life stages: egg, larva, pupa, adult. Examples: caddisflies, midges.

Incomplete metamorphosis life stages: egg, nymph, adult. Examples: stoneflies, mayflies, damselflies, dragonflies.

Important Aquatic Insects of River and Streams

Let's begin with the most important aquatic insect groups which make major contributions to the trout and steelhead diets in rivers and streams, the *moving* water environments. There are many major taxonomical orders of aquatic insects. Here only those of most importance to the nymph angler on most rivers and streams are considered.

Mayflies

For many fly-anglers, the very first aquatic insect considered for identification and study is the mayfly. If a poll was taken, I suspect the mayfly would be the insect selected as the signature fly-fishing logo. Characterized by slender segmented bodies, two or three long wispy tails, and upright wings, mayflies appear as tiny sailboats riding the river currents when their hatching

With hundreds of species, and a broad range of sizes, mayfly adults and nymphs are readily available for trout, char, and steelhead.

time arrives. As with other aquatic insect orders, there are many representatives of the mayfly group, with genera and species numbering in the hundreds worldwide. Sizes and colors vary greatly.

Mayflies have an incomplete life cycle, with three life stages: egg, nymph, and adult.

Nymphs

Mayfly nymphs are characterized by a single wing pad on the top of the thorax, a bulging area where the wings develop and grow. There are two or three tails on an obviously segmented body, and gills are found on the abdomen. A single little hook or claw is located at the end of each leg.

Mayfly nymphs are an important dietary component for fish in both streams and lakes. They all share these identifying characteristics: 2 or 3 slender tails, a single wing pad, and a single claw at the end of each leg.

In moving waters the mayfly genera and species will often segregate themselves by exploiting different specific environments. This is a useful survival mechanism to prevent overcrowding and competition for food. Some nymphs prefer fast water, others slower currents, or backwaters with virtually no current. Some live in stony terrain, while wood debris, vegetation, or silty bottoms are preferred by others. A few mayfly nymphs are adequate swimmers, while many varieties drift helplessly in the current if they should lose their grips on their surroundings during their wanderings.

Knowing that nymphs are poor swimmers, the nymph angler will know to fish mayfly nymphs with a slow "dead-drift" presentation. For flies, I like patterns such as the Hare's Ear, Copper John, Pheasant Tail and my Skinny Minnie May, sizes 12 through 18.

Stoneflies

No matter their size or zip code, adult stoneflies have obviously segmented bodies, two stout tails, two large pairs of wings folded back over the body at rest, and distinctly longer than the body, and two tiny claws at the end of each leg.

*A few stonefly species, like the **Pteronarcys californica**, nicknamed the salmonfly, can measure more than two inches.*

Two stout tails, two wing pads, two tiny claws at the tip of each leg, and feathery gills found on the thorax at the base of the legs will identify the nymph as a stonefly.

Though there are only a few dozen species, they are a significant food source to trout and steelhead in freestone streams, particularly here in the American and Canadian West. Whereas most aquatic insects have a one-year life cycle, some stonefly species may

Because some stonefly nymphs have a three-years-to-adulthood life cycle they are available to river trout and steelhead on a year-round basis.

take three years to reach adulthood. Those that do can be very much larger than their aquatic brethren. The *Pteronarcys californica*, nicknamed the salmonfly, can exceed a length of more than two and one half inches. This is a significant mouthful for even a large fish. Because of their long life cycle, in rivers in which large stoneflies live, the nymphs are available to fish year-round.

Poor swimmers, stonefly nymphs are best fished with a natural dread-drift presentation along the stream bottom. Because of their need for highly oxygenated water, stonefly nymphs are often best fished in and near rapids and riffles where they live among the stones and wood debris. My Princely Stonefly Nymphs, Kaufmann's Rubber Leg Stonefly, and Berry Super Stone patterns are effective for both trout and steelhead. My favorite sizes range from 6-10.

Caddisflies

Adult caddisflies look very much like moths, especially when observed during their bouncing and erratic flight. Observed at rest on riverside limbs or vegetation, these are the characteristics which identify an insect as an adult caddisfly: wings longer than the body, held tent-like over the body at rest. The wings are covered with tiny hairs. There are no tails. The caddisfly is equipped with long antennae, often longer than the body. Worldwide there are thousands of caddisfly species and subspecies. No matter their size and colors, which vary greatly, they all share these same identifiable characteristics.

Nymph anglers will focus on the two immature caddisfly life stages of interest to the fish, the larva and pupa. For those insects which have a complete life cycle, the term "nymph" is not accurate, even though the larvae and pupae are fished using the nymph-fishing method.

Caddisfly Larvae

The caddisfly larva appears as a grub-like worm with a distinct head and tiny antennae, an obvious thorax bearing its six insect legs, and a long segmented abdomen with little hooks at its terminus. Some build cases in which they live and carry with them wherever they travel. The caddis larva constructs its case by cementing items like fir needles, leaf pieces, small stones, and/or assorted bits of vegetation from its environment. When alarmed, the caddis larva will pull its head and legs into its case, like a turtle does when danger is about. Other larvae are free-living case-less roamers who live in the interstitial spaces of the rocks and stream debris. Some of the free-living larvae construct crude sticky nets that trap drifting morsels upon which these insects will dine. Trout and steelhead love caddis larvae, even if they have to swallow the case along with the bug. The digestive juices in the fish's stomach will dissolve the larva so its nutritional value can be utilized. The empty case is then jettisoned once the intestinal passage is complete.

Looking like moths in flight, caddisfly adults are characterized by long antennae (sometimes longer than the body length), absence of tails, and wings at rest which are held tent-like over the body. The wings are distinctly longer than the body.

Across several hundred species, some caddisfly larvae build cases, while others are free-living. Even those with cases will be eaten by trout and steelhead. Digestive juices in the fish's intestinal tract will break down the insect inside the case, providing nutrition.

Removing the caddisfly larva from its case reveals a grub-like insect. As a kid I fished the removed larva as bait on a tiny hook. It was deadly.

As with other aquatic insect orders, sizes and colors exhibit tremendous variety. Some dependable flies to imitate the caddisfly larvae include the Prince Nymph, Peeking Caddis, and the Bead Head Hare Scud.

Caddisfly Pupa

When it's time for the cased caddisfly larva to transition into the next life stage, the cased varieties seal themselves inside the case to soon transform into the pupal stage. The free-living larvae create a bubble-like case in which they make the change. Once the transformation to pupa is complete, the insect will break from its case and make a mad swimming dash for the surface.

Caddisfly pupae are the third stage of the insect's life cycle. Most swim furiously to the surface before the pupal skin is shed at the surface, and the adult emerges. Swimming and swinging nymph flies can be sinfully effective during this emergence.

For the nymph angler, the pupa fly can be fished convincingly using two techniques on the same cast. Initially, the fly is fished with a natural dead-drift. Once the fly line and leader are pulled tight in the current, the fly will ascend toward the surface, mirroring the rise of the actual insect swimming upward to hatch into its adult stage. Bead Head Serendipity, Micro May, Bead Head Soft Hackle, Hotwire Caddis, and my Skinny Minnie Caddis are excellent fly choices, sizes 12-18.

Midges /Chironomids

Midges are ubiquitous little insects, with many thousands of species having been identified, and more than 2,500 in North America alone. Midges are members of a handful of insect families, but it's the Chironomidae family which contains most of the midges that make a big-time contribution to the trout diet in both moving and stillwaters. In the fly-fishing lexicon you will hear "midge", "Chironomid", and "Chironomid midge" used interchangeably.

What midges lack in size they compensate for in numbers, and fish will rise to eat the helpless adults before they fly to safety. Though a staple pattern in lakes and ponds, trout in river back eddies will also feed heavily on them at times.

Adult Chironomids are identified by an obviously segmented body with no tails. Its wings have a delta orientation at rest, and are shorter than the body. The males have bottlebrush antennae which assist them in locating the females at mating time.

Chironomid Larvae

Midges pass through a four-stage life cycle, just like the caddisflies. The larva is an anorexic thin, nine-segment "worm". Some live in tubes in the lake or river bottom, while others are free-roaming nomads, balancing their search for both food and protective cover. These "skinny worms" may be cream-colored, or shades of brown or green. A striking red variety has a hemoglobin-like substance in its body enhancing the ability of the insect to extract oxygen from the water where the oxygen levels can be extremely low. Feeding fish readily recognize the "blood worm" as a desirable snack. Some of my favorite Chironomid larvae flies include the Turbo Worm, V-Rib Larva, and Anorexic Worm.

This largemouth bass fell for an imitation of a midge bloodworm larva.

Chironomid Pupae

Larvae eventually transform into the pupal stage, comma-shaped creatures composed of a thin segmented abdomen, above which is a bulbous head/thorax/developing wing complex, topped by prominent feathery white gill filaments. After their slow ascent to the surface, the pupae transform into winged adults. The adults fly from the surface, swarm, mate, and the female deposits her fertilized eggs back into the water where the life cycle begins anew.

It is the pupal stage of the midge's lifecycle that is of most interest to the fly-angler. Though fishing larval patterns and adult imitations will catch fish, trout naturally focus on the helpless pupae, readily available to be eaten as they are suspended or slowly rising in the water column with no chance to hide or swim for cover. Internally generated gases "inflate" the pupa, giving it a little buoyancy which aids in its slow ascent toward adulthood. It can take several days to create enough gas to enable the rise of the insect toward the surface. In the meantime they remain vulnerably exposed prey for cruising trout.

My Gill Hat, Gunmetal Chironomid, BTW Chironomid, and the Skinny Minnie are seriously good flies when the fish are looking for midge pupae.

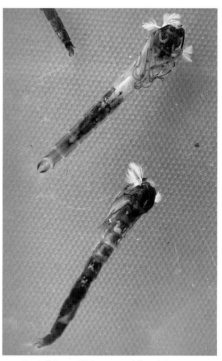

Flies mimicking Chironomid midge pupae are "must" patterns on all stillwaters. Available to be eaten year-round, don't leave home without them.

Important Aquatic Stillwater Insects

There is definitely crossover among some of the orders of important aquatic insects, being significant fish foods in both streams and lakes. Mayflies, caddisflies, and midges are important to trout and other game fish, such as bass, crappie, and bluegill in stillwaters. Midges are extremely important, making up almost 40% of the lake trout's diet in studies conducted by Philip Rowley, a British Columbia angler and writer. Since these crossover insect groups have already been mentioned above, they will not be repeated again in the discussion of stillwater specific bugs.

Even though my reading research indicates that a few species of stoneflies may be found in lakes somewhere in the world, it is very uncommon. I have never discovered a stonefly nymph in a lake or pond, nor have I ever discovered a stonefly in any stomach samples from stillwater fish I have caught.

Dragonflies and Damselflies: Flying Hannibal Lecters

The universally recognized dragonflies, and their close cousins the damselflies, are ferocious predators, both as adults and in their nymphal stages. They are of the insect order Odonata, a word of Greek origin meaning "toothed one". This is a reference to the serrated teeth located on the insect's chewing mouthparts. As adults, they do humankind an excellent service by eating mosquitoes, among other numerous insects on their menu.

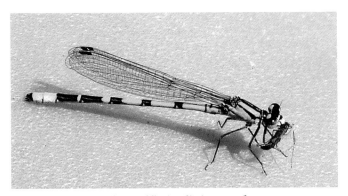

A damselfly in dining mode.

Damselflies and dragonflies undergo incomplete metamorphosis: egg, nymph, adult. Damsels have a life cycle that can range from one to three years, while a dragonfly's can extend to four years. By comparison, the typical mayfly lives for only a few days, and others may live only a few hours.

Adult damselflies can be identified by their long slender abdomens and four membranous wings of identical shape and length that are held back and parallel over the abdomen, unlike the dragonfly which has two pairs of wings that are not identical which are held out to the side of the insect, perpendicular to the body. The dragonfly body is usually much stouter than its cousin. When in flight, the damsel adult appears to be a skinny dragonfly. One more little difference: The eyes of the damsel are separated, while those on most dragonflies touch.

An interesting aside: Dragonflies are among the world's fastest flying insects. In short bursts, they can exceed 30 miles an hour. The world's fastest man, Jamaican Olympian Usain Bolt, topped out at about 28 mph during his fastest 100-meter record time. A very fast

With tremendous vision and lightning-fast flying speed, dragonflies can run down their buggy prey easily. Flying speeds for some species can exceed 30 miles per hour, more than 40 feet per second. This would be breaking the speed limit set in most city neighborhoods; school zones for sure.

dragonfly would have beaten him for the gold medal. That's right, beaten by a bug.

As nymphs, damselflies and dragonflies are equipped with an interesting anatomical structure that covers the mouth called a labial mask. The mask is actually a grasping tool that rests on the insect's face. If a swimming insect or little fish swims near, the "mask" is extended on an arm attached under the predator's head. This move is lightning fast as the prey is nabbed and brought back to those chewing serrated teeth.

Dragonfly Nymphs

Depending on their taxonomic family, the body of the dragonfly nymph ranges from short and rounded to elongated and stout, different than the sleeker damselfly. It is tail-less. Some dragonfly nymphs exceed two inches in length. They have a unique form of locomotion, jet propulsion, and swim in short bursts. This is accomplished when the nymph draws water into its abdomen, then quickly expels it. Imitating this darting movement with short, quick pulls on the fly line makes for a convincing retrieve of a dragon nymph fly.

Dragonfly nymphs can be grouped by their hunting activities and hunting locations. There are crawlers, sprawlers, and burrowers. The crawlers cruise the vegetation and debris on the pond or lake bottom hunting for prey. When needed, they can swim in short, fast bursts to apprehend their food. Whereas the crawlers can be more than 2 inches long, the sprawlers may be half this length. Sprawlers are experts at ambushing their prey, as they hide on the mud and debris of the bottom, camouflaged

As nymphs, dragonflies wait in ambush to dine on passing table fare, including tiny fish. They swim by jet propulsion, a movement pattern important to imitate for successfully fishing dragonfly patterns.

in their surroundings. Covered with tiny hairs which cause bits of their surroundings to cling to their bodies, they make it difficult for unsuspecting wandering or swimming insects, crustaceans, and fish to escape before the labial mask extends to apprehend them. Finally, burrowers bury themselves into the mud and silt to wait in ambush, while at the same time remaining out of sight of predators that might eat them. These are the smallest of the dragonflies, barely an inch long.

Dragonfly nymphs can be black, dark brown and shades of olive, depending on the camouflage requirements of its environment. The fly pattern should be fairly stout, with fly sizes ranging from 6 to 10. The O'Keefe Carey Bugger, my Skinny Minnie Dragon and Stubby Bugger are excellent choices.

Damselfly Nymphs

Damselfly nymphs have pronounced thoraxes, slender abdomens, and three caudal lamellae extending out the rear of the abdomen. The lamellae look like three brushy tails, but are actually gills. As the nymph swims, it's also "breathing", as dissolved oxygen is extracted from the water by the gills.

It is among the stillwater vegetation that damselfly nymphs prefer to hunt and hide. With their extendable lower jaw, they will eat aquatic insect nymphs, larvae, and pupae, small crustaceans, and tiny fish.

Closely related to dragonflies, damsel nymphs are also predators in their youth. Their undulating swimming movement is important for the astute fly-angler to simulate.

Heading for the shore, a protruding log, or lakeside vegetation during their hatching migrations, damselfly nymphs usually swim in the upper three feet of the water column, easily visible to anglers. And, highly visible to hungry fish, too. They have a very distinctive side-to-side undulation of the abdomen as they swim. Swimming bursts are separated by pauses, with short periods of rest before resuming the swim. Simulating this recognizable swim-and-pause movement during the fly retrieve can make for some very memorable fishing.

For damsels I carry patterns in shades and blends of tan, brown, gold, and olive. The Goat Damsel, Marabou Damsel, and the Skinny Minnie Damsel are my mainstays, sizes 8 through 12.

A Non-Insect Fish Food Organism: The Scud

There is a very important food source in both lakes and streams that is fished using the nymph-fishing method: the scud.

Often referred to as freshwater shrimp, scuds are important food sources for lake fish, and in some rivers, too. How significant? In lakes where they are found—and these are numerous—scuds can be second only to Chironomids as a food source. In the fall it can be a dead heat between these two groups as to which will top the list of preferred menu items. Though scuds may be demoted to a secondary food source when insects are active and hatching, they will increase in importance to hungry fish during quiet times.

Though not insects, using various nymphing methods to fish scud flies will add tremendously to the catch in stillwaters and rivers where they are present. Orange spots may be visible in pregnant scuds, and also those infected by a particular parasite. A little orange in a scud fly can be particularly effective.

Scuds have a very distinctive appearance: two pairs of antennae, numerous pairs of leg-like appendages on the underside, and a semi-transparent segmented exoskeleton. Underwater forests of vegetation make for great scud habitat, as do rocky shoals and detritus expanses on the lake or pond bottom. They tend to concentrate along the shallow margins of lakes where sunlight can penetrate to produce abundant plant growth. Camouflage experts, the freshwater shrimp blend with their surroundings, colored in shades of olive, gray, and brown. Scuds molt as they outgrow their old exoskeleton. The freshly molted crustacean will have a bluish pearl appearance for a brief time.

Light sensitive, scuds are typically most active during low light, early morning and evening, and overcast days. They swim slowly in short bursts, and then pause to rest. As they pause, they sink a bit before resuming their travels. Mimicking this alternating swim and rest rhythm during the retrieve is a smart strategy.

The Tied-Down Caddis Shrimp, Plastic-Back Scud, and Bead Head Hare Scud are all good flies, sizes 10 through 18, in shades of olive, olive gray, and brown. A dot of orange dubbing fur to imitate the egg mass carried by female scuds can add a bit of realism to the fly when pregnant females are abundant.

Collecting and Preserving Aquatic Organisms

It is useful to collect aquatic organisms in order to create or purchase fly patterns that are exacting matches of fish foods on a given lake or stream at a particular time of year. An angler can then have high confidence in the flies on subsequent ventures to the same body of water. A rudimentary identification of the insect and non-insect organisms is usually all that is necessary, so there is commonly no need to be overwhelmed with a precise genus and species I.D. Note size, shape, and color of the creature, and, if possible, observe any peculiarities in the way the live critter moves or swims.

The equipment needed to collect and preserve aquatic organisms is simple and inexpensive. A hardware store or big box "mart" store should have everything.

Items needed:
- 36" x 36" fine-mesh netting to be tacked or stapled to two dowel rods
- Tweezers
- Bodkin (a needle on a stick)
- Aquarium net
- Yogurt or cottage cheese container lid
- Lidded glass vials
- Isopropyl (rubbing) alcohol
- Magnifying glass

Holding the netting/dowel rod assembly against the bottom, immediately downstream of your standing position, roll rocks and disturb the substrate with your foot

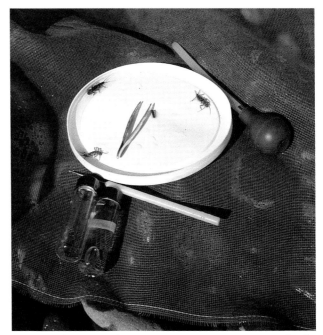

Situated on top of my insect net are a tweezers, bodkin, stomach pump, and preservation vials containing a 50/50 mix of water and rubbing alcohol.

to dislodge the aquatic organisms, which will drift into the net. Take the net ashore to observe what has been caught. Notice in particular what food items might predominate, knowing that these might be the most important creatures to imitate.

Fill the cottage cheese lid with water. Place the organisms of interest on the lid. The water will keep them alive and allow you to observe those with swimming capabilities.

Preservation and Necessary Info

If any organisms are chosen to be kept for future examination, place them in the lidded vials. Prior to placing them in the vials, the vials should be filled with a 50-50 mixture of water and rubbing alcohol. If water alone is used, bacterial action will disintegrate the organism in a matter of a few days. If vial contains only undiluted alcohol, the color will be leached out and insects will become brittle, so antennae, legs, and the head will soon detach.

Some basic information should be recorded. Because their prevalence can be very seasonal, the date when particular insects were collected can be very important. Besides noting the body of water, also record the environment in which the creatures were captured, such as fast, shallow water with a rocky bottom, vegetation along shoreline, or on wood debris in quiet water, and so on.

This information can be easily stored with the preserved specimen. Cut a thin strip of plain white paper that will fit inside the vial with your insect. Using a

Stealing a fish's lunch is a certain means to determine their dining preferences. The fish should be at least 10 inches long to prevent injury. Holding it belly-up makes the fish easier to handle, again, preventing injury from rough handling.

This vial contains Callibaetis *mayfly nymphs collected to observe at leisure the exact size, color, and shape to construct some accurate fly patterns later.*

pencil—not pen—write (tiny print!) the necessary info on the paper strip and put it in the vial. The alcohol and water will not affect the pencil lead, whereas the alcohol will lift ink off the paper. The liquid in the vial would become the color of the ink.

A Collection Method Alternative

With a fish stomach pump you can steal a trout's lunch. The pump looks like a miniature turkey baster and it can be used in one of two ways.

One possibility is to depress the bulb, then gently insert the barrel of the pump into the fish's gullet. As the bulb is allowed to re-inflate by removing the fingers which depressed it, the organisms which the fish has just recently eaten are "vacuumed" up into the barrel. Then the fish is released. Suction some water into the pump, then inject the contents onto the white cottage cheese lid.

As an alternative, water is suctioned into the bulb before inserting the pump barrel into the fish's throat. Some of the water is injected into the fish's stomach, which mixes with the stomach contents. When the bulb is allowed to revert to its natural state the slurry is drawn back into the pump.

It is not unusual to find recently-eaten living insects in the stomach pump sample. I have actually watched insects "stolen" from a fish continue to transform from the nymph or pupal stage into the adult, then fly away. Think Jonah and the whale.

THREE

Nymph-Fishing Equipment Essentials

I t will be a mistake, I think, for veteran anglers to bypass this chapter. Truly effective nymph fishing is all about the details, including the equipment. To suppose any rod, reel, and line will get the job done in all, or even most, situations is not the case, especially across the broad ranges of nymphing for stream trout, stillwater game fish, and steelhead. One size does not fit all. And, it's much more than just knowing to use a light-weight rod for trout and a heavier-weight rod for steelhead.

Rod, reel, fly line, and leader selection would be a simple matter if catching oodles of naïve 10-inch hatchery trout is your ultimate nymph-fishing goal. However, I suspect that virtually all fly-anglers will eventually have higher aspirations. To catch larger, wily fish in public waters every competitive edge is necessary, including equipment needed to get the fly to the fish at various distances and depths, and to successfully bring the hooked fish to hand. Think of the fly rod, reel, fly line, backing, leader, tippet, and fly as instruments in an orchestra. Each has its part to play as fine music is produced. If one instrument does not play its part correctly,

the music is unpleasantly disharmonic, even though all others are playing perfectly. Every component of the nymph-fishing equipment "orchestra" must perform perfectly and in concert with all the others for an angler to be consistently effective, and to, perhaps, land that fish of a lifetime.

Fly Rod Lengths and Matching Fly Line Weights

Fly rods come in a variety of lengths and "fly line weight" designations. Let's examine each with our objective being to find the right rod for you.

Rod lengths range from 6 to 16 feet, with 9 feet being the single most popular for general use. Lake anglers often prefer rods in the 9 1/2- to 10-foot range in order to keep the line off the water on the back cast and to have the fly line a bit more elevated to get more distance on the cast when necessary. These lengths provide the *typical* fly angler—man or woman, child or adult, tall or short, strong or weak—the best combination of casting ease, casting distance, minimum fatigue, and fly line control.

The suggested fly line "weight" inscribed on the fly rod blank indicates the appropriate size or fish species for a particular rod. When the rod is paired with its recommended fly line, the rod's performance can be optimized, and the fly easily presented to a fish at a reasonable distance.

Fly line "weights", and the rods which match them, range from 0-weight through 14-weight. These numbers correspond to an actual physical weight of the tapered portion of a fly line, the first 30 to 40 feet. The *grain* is the unit of weight measure. 1 ounce = about 454 grains.

Here is a general summary of fly line weights/fly rods matched to the typical target species:

- 0 – 3-weight fly lines/fly rods:
  Panfish and small to average trout.
- 4 – 6-weight: Typical trout rods.
- 7 – 9-weight: Typical steelhead, salmon, bass, and light saltwater.
- 10 – 14-weight: Big-species saltwater or mountain rescue.

These classifications are generally accepted guidelines, not hard fast rules. I have landed 8-pound steelhead on 5-weight fly rods and 4-inch trout on a 9-weight. However, it is usually best to select the appropriate rod for the particular species or most likely fish size, though I will suggest some exceptions to consider for stillwater nymphing.

Thoughts on Fly Rods: Rivers vs. Lakes

Because a fly rod for stream and river trout is most likely to be the most straight-forward selection, let's begin there.

During twenty years of fly-fishing retail I sold hundreds and hundreds of fly rods to trout anglers. The single most popular combination of rod length and fly line weight was 9-foot for a 5-weight fly line. I would imagine the same is true today, more than a decade later.

I have a handful of 9-foot 5-weight rods in my personal collection. However, I often cast large, heavily-weighted stonefly nymphs in rivers. Sometimes the wind blows. Even though I may be targeting trout, in many of my Pacific Northwest rivers 5-10-pound steelhead may be in the fish mix at certain times of year, and I may accidently hook one. For all these reasons a 6-weight fly rod is a better match for me. For a little more casting distance when needed, mending the fly line (much more about mending later), and enhanced hook-setting capability I prefer a 9 1/2-foot rod length. So, my Number 1 river nymphing choice: 9 1/2-foot rod for a 6-weight fly line.

As I consider my ideal fly rods for lakes and ponds, choices become more involved. There is such a variety

When both steelhead and trout may be in the summer day's mix, a 6-weight rod is my choice.

of fly and tippet sizes and nymph-fishing methods in stillwaters that it is difficult to make a one-rod selection to effectively meet all the challenges made by fish in this realm.

At the top of my list of lake fishing fly rod selection challenges is dealing with little flies matched to very light tippets. (A *tippet* is the terminal end of a leader, to which the fly is tied. More on tippets soon.) Because quality lakes can produce huge trout that may prefer to dine on tiny insects at times, these fish can be broken off on the strike or during the battle. To cushion a hard strike, and to keep the leader intact during a hard long fight, fly rod *action* needs to be considered.

Rod Action Choices

Rod action refers to the degree to which a rod bends over its entire length when the rod tip is strongly bent, such as when a big fish is on the end of the line. A fast-action fly rod is one where the upper 1/4 to 1/3 of it readily bends, while the lower 2/3 remains straight. A medium-action rod bends to its midpoint, while a slow, or full-flex, rod flexes all the way to the grip. Each has its plusses and minuses. Each has its advocates and detractors.

Too many inexperienced fly-anglers think that a fast-action fly rod is the best choice. You know: fast horses, fast cars, fast times, fast-action fly rod. Because the rod tip recovers quickly to its unbent "resting" position, the fast-action rod is capable of shooting a fly line at higher velocities, resulting in greater casting distance. However, just like driving a Ferrari at high speeds through

As my clients, many of them inexperienced, fight a large fish I watch the rod tip for my coaching suggestions. I always want a solid bend in the rod, with no fingers on the line or reel, except when reeling line.

mountain turns, timing and control become critical issues. Experienced casters can master the timing stroke and cast a long beautiful line. Others muscle or mis-time the casting rhythm of a fast rod, which results in a poor cast. So, fast may not be the best choice for all casters. Additionally, a fast, quick-responding rod tip can easily break a light tippet when the angler sets the hook with too much enthusiasm.

In contrast to the fast, tip-action rod, there is the slow or full-flex rod. The rod-bend recovery of the tip takes longer than the other actions, and the casting stroke is much slower. The more casual recovery of the tip allows the caster more time to feel the flex in the rod, to better get a sense for the casting mechanics. Relaxed calm is a good mental approach with this action type. Best to think of casting this rod type as a slow, sensual dance.

The full-flex rod action reduces the possibility of breaking off a fish on the strike or during the fight. Much like a forgiving shock absorber, the impact of a hard strike or overly-powerful hook-set against resistance is cushioned. While trying to wrestle a worthy fish into submission, even a heavy-handed impatient angler will have a lesser chance of losing his fly and the fish. No guarantee, but a better chance.

Most fly rods will fall into the medium-action category, flexing most down to their mid sections. Think of a fast-action and a slow-action model, then, split the action difference. It is here that most fly-anglers will settle with their choices when it comes to selecting a fly rod. This is okay, and probably a logical choice until an urgent need is perceived.

Productive lakes can produce many more 20-plus-inch fish than most rivers, so it's difficult for me to choose a single ideal fly rod for fishing lakes and ponds where big fish swim. Also, I commonly use three different nymph-fishing methods on lakes, where one nymphing technique predominates on rivers. When I troll small nymphs on light tippets in lakes with extra-large fish, my line is tight. I must depend on the soft, full-flex rod tip to cushion a high-impact strike from quality fish. To accomplish this end, I use a 3- or 4-weight rod with a soft tip. Rod length is irrelevant when I troll since it is not necessary to make long casts, or even cast at all, since I can merely strip line from my reel and swim or paddle away from it. So my ideal nymph trolling lake rod is one that does not follow the general guidelines for matching rod/fly line-weight to the recommended fish size. I use an 8-foot – 9-foot 3-weight or 4-weight model.

Note: *For a rod strictly used for trolling*, with minimal casting needs, big-box stores carry inexpensive slow-action fly rods that will work just fine, making a second fly rod quite reasonable. However, NEVER skimp on a fly reel used for playing big fish.

A Couple of Issues to be Considered

An obvious question: Will a big fish break a lightweight rod? Most modern graphite fly rods can be flexed hard with little risk of breaking. If the angler fears for his bent rod during the fight with a bruiser merely change the angle at which the rod is held, decreasing the amount of bend. To remove all flex, point the rod directly at the fish. Then there is absolutely no bend and stress on the rod whatsoever. When you do this, expect the fish to break your tippet since there is no longer any shock absorption by the rod tip.

A second consideration: Will playing a large fish, which will be released, on a very light rod perhaps fatigue the fish to the point it cannot recover? Isn't it

necessary to play a big fish quickly on a heavier weight rod? If the water temperature is 70 degrees Fahrenheit, or higher, the amount of dissolved oxygen available to trout can be dangerously low. If the fish is seriously stressed it may not be able to absorb the needed oxygen quickly enough to survive. The logical decision here is not to fish, even if you use a heavier-weight rod to play the fish quickly. The fish is still played to exhaustion in order to land and release it. I think rod weight is not a consideration.

When water temperatures are cold to moderate, and dissolved oxygen levels are good, I do not believe any harm is done to a fish that is played and released on a lightweight rod. It is not logical that a fish with cool or moderate temperatures will not recover if the fish is handled gently and "revived" before its release to fight another day. You and I will not run up a hill at high speed until our hearts explode. At least I won't. As I get fatigued I will slow down or stop. Fish do the same, even during the trauma of fighting against a fishing line. To help the fish recover before release, hold it gently upright in the water, moving it slowly back and forth to assist in getting oxygenated water flowing past the gills. The revived fish will eventually swim out of your hand on its own accord.

For casting and retrieving nymphs on lakes and ponds, I will choose a 9-foot – 9 1/2-foot 5-weight fly rod with a slow or medium action. If I will be casting larger nymphs, especially in wind, I will opt for a 6-weight rod with a medium action. Because I will be using a stronger tippet with a larger fly, I do not need the same degree of shock absorption required by small flies and light tippets.

For those who do not have the means or the inclination to accumulate an entire arsenal of rods, I recommend the fly-angler figure a compromise.

Steelhead Fly Rods

Fly rods casting 7-, 8-, or 9-weight fly lines are best suited for steelhead, sea-going rainbow trout which typically grow to 6 to 10 pounds in their adulthood, though steelhead over 30 pounds have been caught on a rod and reel. Eight-weight rods are most commonly used.

The decision-making for a rod purchaser comes with determining the rod length. For many years a 9- or 10-foot steelhead fly rod was standard. In 1980's there was a big move toward two-hand rods typically measuring 13 – 14 feet. Besides being fun to cast, these long rods make for very long casts with little effort and excellent line-mending capability.

The new century saw the advent of a tremendous

popularity in "switch" rods, those to be cast with one or two hands. Switch rods are usually 11 to 12 feet long, a compromise between the more traditional 9- – 10-foot one-hand rods and the much longer two-hand, or Spey, rod.

Solved: Casting and Mending Challenges

Many fly-rodders are nuts for steelhead here in the Pacific Northwest, including me, and including most of my fishing clients. Though some will debate me, steelhead are the most exciting freshwater game fish to be caught on a fly rod. Many salmon are bigger, but the excitement of a jumping silver bullet and the satisfaction of meeting the challenges to even hook this fish are unparalleled.

Two-hand rods have been tremendously popular for steelhead for years, but now more trout anglers, especially nymphers, use 5- and 6-weight two-hand rods for river trout.

My challenge is enabling my clients to catch steelhead on a fly rod ... even those clients who have no fly-fishing skills! Often I have to take an inexperienced angler, enable them to make a reasonable cast, manipulate the line to get a convincing drift of the fly, detect the strike, set the hook properly, and enable them to play that fish to the net. Many years ago the solution to how to accomplish all of this came to me, and it's been a good one.

In nymph fishing, a standard fly cast is commonly not used. The fly line is lifted, then slung or lobbed to the target. Not classically beautiful, but effective. With weighted flies or weight attached to the leader it can be very dangerous to attempt a standard fly cast with the line passing back and forth, in front of, then behind the angler. If you attempt this with heavy nymphs, or are standing within the same zip code of someone trying this, you had better be wearing a welder's mask and bulletproof body armor.

My solution is to use a two-hand rod measuring 13 – 14 feet for nymphing steelhead.

Hey, Hey! Oh, My!
Steelhead Want a Nymphing Fly

I just heard the thud of some fly-fishing purists hit the floor as they fainted. Two-hand rods were designed to gracefully cast wet flies, not fling a nymph! There are anglers who take affront at the marriage of two-hand rods and nymph fishing, but there are plenty of steelhead that want only a fly presented via nymphing technique and we will gladly take those fish.

Stonefly imitations, even those who don't bear a close resemblance to the actual colors of real insects, can be very effective for steelhead.

Three Questions

In my book *Steelhead Fly Angling: Guerilla Fly Rod Tactics* I posed three questions to be answered when it comes to any fly-fishing technique and the particular equipment used to employ it:

1. Are the method and gear legal?
2. Are the method and gear sporting?
3. Do you enjoy using the method and gear to catch fish?

If "Yes!" is the answer to all of these questions, then get out there and have fun!

Minimal Skills and Excellent Effectiveness

Over my many years as a fly-fishing guide I have enabled unskilled teenagers and non-fishing spouses to catch the elusive steelhead on a fly rod. This is no small feat when there is only one fishing day in which to accomplish this. It is the capabilities of a lengthy two-hand rod which allow this. With a very long rod the line is kept high in the air, above the heads of the anglers and boatman. Once on the water, the fly line can be mended easily when simple

instructions are followed. When it's time to set the hook, such a long lever allows for a sudden and long sweep of the line to tighten it against the fish. All these necessary actions are made possible by a rod measuring in double-digit feet.

My recommendation for the ultimate steelhead nymph fishing fly rod: 13- – 14-foot medium-action rod matched with a 7- or 8-weight fly line.

One More Rod Consideration

Always try casting a rod before buying it. Just because a rod is expensive does not mean it will suit your casting and fishing needs. Just as you would not usually buy a car before a test drive, consider casting the rod before you plunk down a few hundred dollars. If a friend has a similar rod, taking it for a spin on the lawn or on the water is no problem. If this is not an option, specialty fly-fishing stores typically allow prospective buyers to cast any rod on the rack.

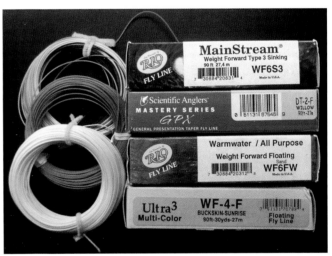

A brightly-colored, weight-forward taper fly line is always my choice for indicator nymphing.

Choosing the Right Fly Line

With so many, many choices for fly lines, I will attempt here to simplify the selection process.

Fly lines float, sink, or the tip of the line sinks and the remainder floats. They come in a vast array of colors. Standard fly lines are tapered so they lay out fairly straight when properly cast.

Nymphing Fly Lines,
Rivers & Streams vs. Stillwaters

When nymph fishing in moving waters, I use a floating line 100% of the time. Seems counterintuitive, doesn't it? Even though I am fishing my flies very near the bottom

Two-hand rods make casting easy, effective mending a breeze, and the sweep of the fly line on the hook-set cannot possibly be matched by a shorter one-hand rod.

of the stream, I rely on a *visual* indication that a fish has intercepted my fly, not trusting to feel the strike before the fish expels my nymph.

During graduate school at Oregon State University, I did a project for my Comparative Animal Behavior class. I watched cutthroat trout through a Plexiglas window from a small room built into the side of Berry Creek. It was very instructive. Some key observations: Trout are always on the lookout for something to eat. They will examine anything and everything that drifts into their visual zone, even those items that are obviously not edible, such as fir needles, leaf bits, and tiny pieces of wood. When a hungry fish would inhale a fir needle or other little bit of non-edible debris, they would quickly expel it. The interception and the expulsion could happen in less than a second, a miniscule amount of time. Envision the same happening to an artificial fly. Once a fish detects that the artificial is not a tasty morsel it immediately spits it out. The point here is that a nymph-angler has very little time to detect and react to a strike.

Everything in a fish's immediate surroundings is drifting by at the same speed. It can be alarming if an angler's fly outpaces or under-paces the other flotsam and jetsam drifting by the fish. So, as closely as

possible, the nymph must usually be presented to the fish at a natural drifting speed, the same velocity as everything else passing by. It is logical, then, that there must be slack in the line/leader system so the velocity of the nymph is neither accelerated nor hindered by a tight line. Therefore, since a fish may hold an artificial fly for such a brief instant, by the time the slack in the leader and *sinking* fly line tightens enough to feel the strike, the biting fish is long gone. Instead the hesitation or dip or zip in the tip of a floating fly line, or the

Underwater observations of cutthroat trout during my graduate school years taught me much about fish behavior, making me a much better nymph angler.

interference of the drift of a floating strike indicator, tells the fisherman that the fly may have been grabbed by a fish. So, the strike detection is visual, not tactile. Yes, there are times when a fish will grab a nymph hard when the line comes tight, and there are even times when trout and steelhead may actually prefer a nymph swinging on a tight line at the end of the drift, but a floating line actually allows for the fishing of two nymphing techniques on one drift of the fly: natural dead-drift and a tight-line rise and swing of the nymph.

Since the strike may be evident in the floating fly line, it makes good sense that the line should be a high-visibility color: bright yellow, orange, red, or green. Take your pick. And, no, a bright line does not startle the fish. It's the shadow and splash of the fly line that alerts them.

New Zealand anglers are very skeptical of brightly colored fly lines. I have been there twice and fished with three different professional guides. All frowned at the thought of me using a hi-vis fly line. I assured them I would be responsible for my own fishing success fate. I did quite well on all my guided fishing days. None of the guides mentioned my choice in fly line a second time. Would I have caught more fish with a dull-colored fly line? Frankly, I think not. For my own knowledge I did have a dull olive floating fly line which I used from time to time in NZ. I could perceive no difference in my catch rate, including casting to visible browns and rainbows in shallow water.

Taper Choices

There are two general fly line tapers to consider. Though there are choices within these choices, I will address — generally — the Double-Taper and Weight-Forward taper. Their profiles are quite different, and so are their advantages.

Advantages of the Double-Taper fly line:
1. Smooth and easy roll cast, whereby the line is propelled forward without a back cast.
2. Delicate presentation for a soft landing of the fly.
3. Economy. Tapered at both ends. When the coating on one tapered end wears out, the line can be reversed on the reel to use the unworn second taper.

Advantages of the Weight-Forward taper fly line:
1. Long-distance casts.
2. Better accuracy and distance in the wind.
3. Better for casting large, air-resistant flies and heavy nymphs.

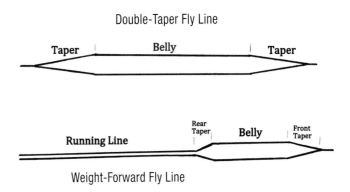

4. The rod loads (flexes) sooner for beginners who initially cast short distances.

My recommendation for a fly line to fish nymphs in rivers and streams: a weight-forward, high-visibility floating fly line.

Stillwater Fly Lines

In addition to my floating fly line, there are three others I use for lake and pond fishing. I will list and discuss each in order of their importance.

Sinking fly lines have varying sink rates, and are designated as Type I, Type 2, through Type VII.

The slowest sinking, Type I, also referred to as an intermediate sinking fly line, descends through the water column at a rate of about 1 1/4 to 2 feet per second. The line is available in a clear finish, no coloration, which adds a small, but important, degree of stealth when dealing with gin-clear water and wary fish. When fish are in shallow water I rely on using my floating fly line and a lightly weighted fly. However, when there is a breeze the floating fly line develops a bow created by the wind-generated surface currents, making subtle strike detection challenging. The intermediate fly line descends below the influence of the breeze to maintain a straight line contact with the fly, but does not descend too quickly to put the nymph on the bottom where it will be dragged through the silt and vegetation and be of no interest to the fish.

In water 15 feet and deeper I use a Type III density-compensated sinking fly line, which drops at a rate of 2 1/2 – 3 1/2 feet per second. A density-compensated line is one that sinks in a straight line. One which is not "compensated" descends in a shallow "U" orientation, whereby an angler is not in good contact with the fly, making the detection of a soft strike difficult. It's worth the extra cost. As for color, charcoal, navy, and dark olive are all suitable choices.

The fourth stillwater fly line in my arsenal is a floating fly line with a 15-foot clear intermediate sinking tip. If the breeze is slight and I need a little more depth than my floating line affords me, I use this line. I like two things about this line — it's easier to pick up off the water to re-cast than a full sinking fly line, and the hi-vis floating portion acts as an elongated strike indicator, allowing me to detect a quiet interception of my fly.

With rare exception, all sinking and sink-tip lines have a weight-forward taper.

WF = weight forward taper	WF-6-S
6 = fly line/rod weight	TYPE III
S = sinking	
Type III = sink rate (2.5-3.5 ips)	2.50-3.50 ips
ips = inches per second	90 ft / 27 m

In addition to the standard specs, discover if a sinking fly line is density-compensated so it descends in a straight line. Without this characteristic a medium or fast-sinking line will descend in a "U" orientation, making strike detection and hook-setting more difficult.

Have an Insurance Policy

There's always a chance that a strong fish will pull all of the fly line from the reel during a long, hard run. In preparation for this event, a backing should be spooled onto the reel before tying on the fly line.

The most commonly used backing line is braided Dacron. It comes in a range of breaking strengths: 12, 20, and 30 pound. For trout fishing I use 50 yards of 20 pound, and for steelhead fishing I prefer 100 yards of 30 pound.

Why braided Dacron? Three reasons: it is very strong for its small diameter; it does not significantly deteriorate with time, including reasonable exposure to sunlight; and lastly, it has very little stretch as a big fish is reeled in under tension, whereas a stretchy line like monofilament can deform a reel spool when many, many tight turns of line seek to return to their "relaxed" state.

The Deals About Reels

Do not ever, ever, ever settle for a mediocre reel with a mediocre drag. Ever!

Once a worthy fish is on the end of the line the one piece of equipment that will usually have the greatest bearing on the success or failure of the battle is the fly reel. If the drag resistance is set correctly and the reel releases the fly line smoothly at high speed, if the hook

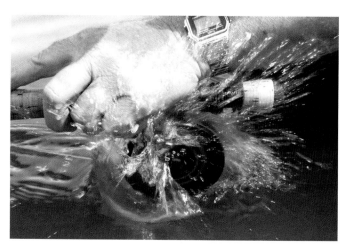

My top requirement in a quality fly reel is that the drag be creamy smooth and perform reliably even when wet.

stays in the fish odds are great it will be landed.

It's all about the drag. A quality, reliable-even-when-wet drag.

There are a variety of fly-reel drag systems. The least expensive is the spring and pawl type, also referred to as the click and pawl. A flat spring applies tension to a triangular tooth, the pawl, which fits into a gear on the reel spool. The possibility of a line overrun is likely with a large fish sprinting away at high speed because this drag is not capable of sufficient resistance, having a low maximum threshold.

The *disc* drag is a common design. There are good ones; there are bad ones. There is not necessarily a good correlation between cost and quality. I have had some very handsomely priced disc-drag reels that failed to perform under stress, either binding up or going to drag-less free-spool. The acid test is how the drag performs when the reel and its inner workings get wet.

The difficulty in purchasing a reel, even a popular brand name, is being able to try it out before it's purchased. The best buying strategy is to extract a promise from the seller that the reel is returnable if the drag does not work as needed.

Size Matters

Most reels come in a variety of sizes. Each reel has its capacity (fly line and backing) detailed. Once the particular fly line and the amount of backing needed for the particular game fish being sought is decided, the fly-reel of the correct size can be determined. Know that reel capacities can be overstated. For this reason, if the capacity of a given reel is very close to, or slightly smaller than, what is needed, opt for the next largest reel size. It's like shoes, better too large than too small.

Knowing the matched fly line and the amount of backing needed will dictate the appropriate reel size. Capacity specs can be found in or on the reel box, or in the manufacturer's literature.

number and whole number in the inches measurement is added, the sum is 11.

Example: 4X = 0.007" 4 + 7 = 11

Tippet Diameter; "X" number; Diameter in inches
0X 0.011"
1X 0.010"
2X 0.009"
3X 0.008"
4X 0.007"
5X 0.006"
6X 0.005"
7X 0.004"
8X 0.003"

It's a Fine Line: Leaders and Tippets

Of all the equipment details that have evolved last in fine-tuning my nymphing system, especially in rivers, it's been leader design. Leader specs are critical elements of my nymph-fishing success.

For years I fished nymphs by modifying a standard out-of-the-package tapered leader, and I continue to do so for much of my stillwater nymphing. Just like fly lines, leaders are tapered so they lay out generally straight, full length, when properly cast. Though there are some shorter and longer than these, packaged tapered leaders are most commonly available in lengths of 7 1/2, 9, and 12 feet, with 9 feet being the most commonly used. A typical profile of a 9-foot leader begins with a large-diameter butt section ranging from 0.020" to 0.025". Over the first 6 1/2 to 7 feet the leader diameter gets progressively smaller. The final 2 – 2 1/2 feet are of uniform diameter. It is this terminal *un-tapered* portion of the leader which is referred to as the *tippet*.

A Critical Math Lesson

In addition to specifying its length there is another important spec on the leader package. It's the "X" number. The "X" number is a reference to the *diameter* of the tippet. And, every fly-angler who aspires to be a deadly-effective nympher must understand this important measurement.

Tippets come in a variety of diameters, and must be matched to the hook size of the fly size being used, balancing both the natural "swimability" of the fly with the appropriate diameter ("X" number) which is adequate to fully extend the leader and fly on a good cast. The following table shows the diameters of commonly used tippet sizes, measured in terms of "X" number, commonly found labeled on leader and tippet packaging, and an equivalent diameter measured in inches. When the "X"

There is an inverse relationship here: the larger the "X" number, the smaller the diameter; the smaller the "X" number, the larger the diameter. The diameter of a 7X tippet is smaller than the diameter of a 3X tippet.

Again, the key to getting the right combination of line extension during the cast, coupled with an effective drift of the fly once it hits the water, lies in the diameter of the tippet. For matching the tippet diameter to the fly size, do the following math:

$$\frac{\text{Fly (hook) size}}{3} = \text{appropriate "X" number}$$

Dime thickness = .053"
0X diameter = .011"
0X is about 1/5 of a dime thickness

A tapered leader's length is naturally reduced by changing flies or breaking the leader on a lost fish or casting into trees. To replenish the length, take a length of tippet line from a spare spool and tie it to the shortened leader with a Double Surgeon's knot.

Leaders and tippets are available in an assortment of line chemistries: monofilament, copolymer, first-generation fluorocarbon, and second-generation fluorocarbon. Without getting too technical, monofilament leaders and tippets are cheapest and have the lowest breaking strength for their diameter; copolymer types are more expensive, but up to 50% stronger; the latest generation fluorocarbon lines are as strong as the copolymers, have significant "invisibility", and are three to four times as expensive as the copolymer.

Leaders & Tippets: My Preferences

For nymphing I gravitate toward supple, soft leaders for minimal influence on the natural action of the fly on or in the water. Even with a soft butt section, my casts lay out generally straight at all distances, even in a significant breeze.

Because fluorocarbon tends to be stiff, I prefer a copolymer tapered leader. I snip off the tippet portion of the leader and replace it with fluorocarbon tippet. In the tippet, I am sacrificing a little suppleness for invisibility.

Losing a worthy fish to an unexplainable break-off is disheartening. Not all second-generation tippet materials are of the same quality. If you experience too many break-offs, try a different brand. Because new and better items come to market all the time, you may discover something more to your liking.

I prefer fluorocarbon's "invisibility" factor. This, I think, is imperative in clear water where wary fish are on high alert. Plenty of stillwater fish succumbed to my flies before fluorocarbon tippets and leaders. However, at the end of a lean or — yikes! — fishless day, I do not want to wonder if a willing biter would have struck a hook if only I had used fluorocarbon. To remove this doubt is important. The type of tippet is under my control, a variable in the fishing success equation I do not want to reflect on. There are too many other factors I cannot control. Even though fluorocarbon is expensive, it is a small cost in comparison to the much larger costs of my other equipment, including rods, reels, waders, boat, and travel. I might use $2 – $3 of tippet in a day. Keep perspective.

The "X" number found on a tippet spool and leader packaging is a reference to diameter. If you look closer at the labeling, you will usually discover the translation into inches. Example: 2X = 0.009". Using the equation above for common stillwater flies, you will probably find 3X, 4X, 5X, and 6X tippets to be the most useful diameters.

Just as with the "X" number and the corresponding measurement in inches, there is an inverse relationship between the hook size number and the actual physical size of the hook. That is, the larger the hook number the smaller the hook's measurable size, specifically the measurement between the main body of the hook (the shank) and the point of the hook. This is a measurement of the hook's gap or gape. Example: a #8 hook is larger than a #14 hook.

In challenging clear-water conditions, I will often give up cast-ability for a better drift or swim of the fly, and tippet invisibility. Instead of using a 4X tippet suggested by my mathematical formula for a #12 fly, I may, instead, use a smaller 5X or 6X diameter so there's a diminished chance a sharp-eyed trout will be able to spy a line attached to my nymph.

The Exacting Specifics of Nymphing Leaders

The nymphing leaders I use in specific situations in both moving and stillwaters are so important I can't do them justice in a few paragraphs. "One size fits all" has no place here. Effective leader specs and construction details are much more involved than just tying on a tapered leader and beginning to fish. Nymphing leaders I use and recommend merit a chapter of their own in the pages that follow.

Strike Indicators

When nymphing moving waters so that the fly drifts naturally — "dead-drift" — with the current, a fish usually moves into position to intercept the artificial; it merely stops it, not tugging on the line and pulling the system tight to signal a strike. It takes no longer than a brief second for the fish to realize it has made a mistake, and quickly release the fake. So, the indication of the typical strike is a matter of *seeing* it happen in the line, not feeling it, most of the time. Those with sharp eyes and mad skills may observe a hesitation or disturbance in the leader or fly line. In fact, some floating "nymphing" fly lines have a brightly colored tip to aid in seeing the strike. I have used such lines, and they work adequately when the cast is short and the light is good. However, weighted flies will sink the tip, or the tip sinks as the line suffers age and wear and tear. Even when new it is hard to detect soft strikes when long casts are required. In these cases I much prefer a hi-vis strike indicator attached to my leader.

When suspending flies motionless off the lake bottom so that they do not sink into the mud or vegetation, a small floating indicator is indispensable . . . and dirty

Greg Schuerger knows about effective nymphing for steelhead.

effective. There are many strike indicator designs and materials. I have used them all in my career. Currently, I usually prefer a soft plastic bubble with a tiny grommet for securing it to the leader. These come in four sizes. I use all but the largest, determined by visibility conditions, fly sizes, and the amount of weight in the flies.

When I must suspend flies in stillwaters deeper than ten feet, I rely on a foam slip-strike indicator. It must break free of its purchase on the long leader, sliding down the line toward the fish. Without sliding down the leader it is very difficult, if not impossible, to land the fish as a firmly fixed indicator can only be reeled in no farther than the rod's tiptop. Imagine a 9-foot fly rod and a 20-foot leader.

In the chapters dealing with leaders the exacting details of securing and the placement of indicators is discussed.

The soft-plastic bubble indicators are a top choice of many nymph anglers. Besides floating without fail, they are available in various sizes and hi-vis colors.

FOUR

River Nymphing Leaders: Construction and Specs

Just as the Devil is found in the details, so is the construction of leaders for effective nymph fishing. For those who would choose to ignore the details here, the price will be paid in fish that could have been caught, but were not.

In addition to the critical specifications for the leader line lengths and diameters, there are important details here about dropper lines, weighting, and strike indicators, all necessary components of a good nymph leader set-up. With rare exception I am fishing multiple flies, two most of the time, but sometimes three in Oregon. How to effectively locate and secure a dropper fly will be discussed and illustrated. Where it is legal, I may attach removable split shot to the leader. Correctly weighted flies will be used when split shot is not allowed. I will explain logical fly pairings and how to know when the right amount of weight can be confirmed. A strike indicator on the upper portion of the leader is critical for strike detection. Indicators of choice and where exactly it should be secured to the leader in relation to the flies will be discussed in this chapter, too.

In all cases in rivers and streams I use a weight-forward floating fly line. Initially it seems counterintuitive that a floating line is used to fish flies near the stream bottom. Why not use a sinking fly line?

As mentioned earlier, when I did underwater observations of feeding trout it became quickly apparent that non-edible items like my artificial flies are held only a

brief moment — sometimes less than a second — before the fish expels them. If a sinking fly line is used to get the flies near the bottom, slack must be kept in the line leader system in order to get a natural dead-drift of the nymphs. There is not enough time between the moment a fish intercepts the fly and releases it for the slack in the line and leader to be pulled tight so the angler knows a fish has grabbed it. It would not be known that a fish had actually bit the fly. Instead, the quickest manner in which we can know a fish has grabbed the nymph is visually, seeing an interruption in the drift of the floating strike indicator. The fly line is seldom pulled tight so the strike can be felt. In the vast, vast majority of cases fish do not hold the fly long enough for this to happen. The indicator signals the strike.

For those who might balk at using a strike indicator the best hope is to focus on the tip of a highly visible floating fly line. There are "nymph tip" fly lines where the first foot or 18 inches is a different color than the main body of the fly line, so the angler has a distinctive focal point at which to see a strike. I have used such

Nymph Set-Up

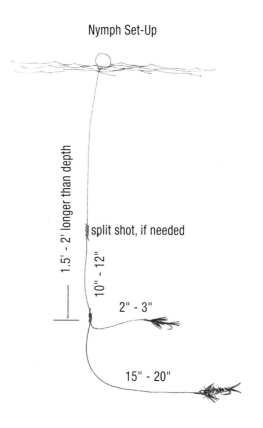

1.5' - 2' longer than depth

10" - 12"

split shot, if needed

2" - 3"

15" - 20"

Quick reactions are usually necessary to hook the fish when the indicator signals a strike. One of the nympher's challenges is to not use too much force on the hook-set. Be fast, but don't be strong.

lines and caught fish with them. However, a good strike indicator attached to the leader is much better at revealing subtle strikes, those interceptions that are difficult, if not impossible, to discern in even a hi-vis fly line. For me, and for my clients, there will always be a strike indicator on the leader for maximum nymphing results.

Leaders for Moving Water

First to be examined will be nymphing leaders for moving water. The second, and much more expansive group of nymphing leaders, will be for stillwater fishing. In all nymphing situations I am looking to balance cast-ability with sink-ability, whereby the leader extends reasonably straight out on the cast and the fly sinks quickly into the target zone.

Though I will use a packaged tapered leader for wet-fly and dry-fly fishing in rivers, I construct my nymphing leaders from scratch. The major concern I have with an extruded leader bought at my local fly shop is that the butt section (the upper portion tied to the fly line) is too large in diameter. Because the current speeds in a river's water column are faster near the surface and much slower near the stream bottom, the fly line and upper portion of the leader are on or near the surface, always racing ahead of, and pulling with them, the nymphs.

Two "Recent" Leader Construction Epiphanies

The butt section of a standard tapered leader has a relatively large diameter compared to the much thinner tippet to which the flies are tied. The larger its profile, the more easily the line is pushed by the current, compared to the current's push on a thin, small-diameter line. I seek to minimize the pulling influence of the leader on my

Mark Kaczmarek nymphs the Rogue River for steelhead. A stonefly nymph paired with a smaller fly or egg pattern on a dropper is an effective combo wherever summer steelhead swim.

nymphs, which allows my flies to sink faster into the target zone near the bottom. Once there, I am attempting to drift the flies slowly and naturally along the bottom, and to delay as long as I can the dragging of my nymphs as the fly line and upper leader move quickly ahead of them.

Properly mending the fly line and upper portion of the leader is what allows for the natural drift of slow-moving nymphs. The mend is a bit more effective, and its beneficial effects a bit longer lasting, with a thinner leader butt section. This has become more important in recent years, especially in steelhead nymph fishing in a competitive environment with intense competition from other anglers trying to catch these prized fish. And, there are seasons when the steelhead numbers in the rivers I frequent are low. Both of these make it necessary to exploit any fish that might be remotely interested in eating an artificial fly. For those steelhead (or worthy lunker trout) that demand the most precise possible presentation of the nymph, seek to discover every little detail which contributes toward this end. A thinner leader butt is such a detail.

The second recent adjustment of significant importance for me has been leader length. Longer is better.

The ideal water depth range for river trout is 3 to 7 feet. Yes, trout can be found in shallower and deeper water than this range, but I recommend beginners focus on this range for the best chance of success. Trout in water less than waist deep are easily alarmed, and if maximum stealth is not employed the fish will bolt from the area with the slightest disturbance. The rookie nympher may erroneously conclude that his methods, leader set-up, or flies are at fault, when in reality there are no fish in his shallow-water fishing zone.

As for water deeper than about 7 feet the leader will most likely need to be lengthened. Discipline and time are required to make the necessary adjustment, and a longer leader will definitely be more cumbersome to cast well, especially with a single-hand rod. Also, in deeper water it may be more difficult to get a convincing drift of the fly, detect the strike, and remove the necessary leader and line slack to set the hook. To effectively fish 7 feet of moving water, use a leader of approximately 11 feet fishing two flies.

Effective moving-water nymph leaders are longer than you might think because the leader is not usually vertical in the water column and you also need to allow for slack in the system to keep the flies drifting naturally. These two things contribute to the necessity for long leaders. If forced to make a choice, always opt for a leader which is too long over one which is too short.

Stream Nymph Leader Specs

In constructing my own nymph leader, I start with a 4 1/2-foot section of 0.017-inch monofilament or copolymer line. As for color, I use a soft green or tan. Using a double surgeon's knot I secure 18 inches of 0.015-inch diameter to the butt section. Then, 18 inches of 0.011" (0X) fluorocarbon line. From here on, the line diameters and lengths depend on the conditions and what species I am trying to catch.

The single most common terminal tippet diameters I use for stream trout are 3X and 4X. I understand that readers may have different needs or preferences. 5X and 6X tippets usually require the insertion of a

transition line segment of 3X diameter between the 0X section of line and these smaller tippets. If 1X and 2X tippet diameters are preferred, these make up the entirety of the final 3 1/2 feet. All leader sections 0X and smaller are second-generation fluorocarbon for maximum invisibility and breaking strength.

The key variable length in my leader set-up is the distance between the strike indicator and the dropper fly. If you fish a single fly then it is the distance from the indicator to your nymph. The depth of the water is constantly different from place to place as you fish throughout the day. For maximum effectiveness, relocate the indicator on the leader, moving it up or down as necessary. Ideally, the indicator will be 1 1/2 – 2 feet farther from my dropper than the water depth. As an example, in 7 feet of water my strike indicator will be 9 feet from the dropper fly. If the fly is never dragging or occasionally hung up on the bottom, I will continue to lengthen this distance. Again, better too long than too short.

The Dropper Fly

I lost the biggest steelhead of my life because I was fishing two flies. It was on British Columbia's Babine River in the late 1980's, when two flies could, apparently, be legally used. At least none of the guides I fished with at the time told me any differently. My guide for the day estimated that the fish I had tired to the point it was resting a rod length from me in the surface, just out of reach, was greatly fatigued. The guide actually touched the fish on the tail several times with the landing net, but was unable to make the scoop because the bottom was silty and overhanging bushes extending to the river's edge for a long distance in both directions did not allow the possibility of beaching the huge steelhead we estimated at 24 – 25 pounds.

As my prize swam for long minutes to and fro, always staying just beyond the net, it eventually found a submerged stick on which it hung my dropper fly, a #4 Skykomish Sunset, the fly which will forever live in infamy for me. The fly did not break off immediately, but I knew the inevitable outcome. Finally, the behemoth buck slowly finned laterally away from me, toward the middle of the river. It did not panic and bolt when it felt the unyielding tension of the wood. It moved painfully slowly away until the leader snapped, then he

River Nymphing Leader

Fly Line	4 1/2'	18"	18"	12"	12"	18"
Strike Indicator	0.017" diameter	0.015"	0X	3X / Split Shot		

tippet rings

├── 3X, 4X, or 5X ──┤

├────── 1X or 2X for Steelhead ──────┤

It's imperative that the dropper line be short to prevent the dropper fly from wrapping around or tangling with the main leader.

With this dropper set-up, when a fish noses the line it may be startled and turn away, or push the line and miss the fly.

faded into the depths wearing my purple Spey fly in its jaw. I still have nightmares.

I continue to fish multiple flies for steelhead, willing to risk the same scene I had on the Babine. And the Deschutes. And the Rogue River. And the South Santiam. And . . .

Multiple flies on the leader give picky fish a choice. Also, if one of the flies does not drift close enough to interest a trout or steelhead, the second fly may do so. Two or three flies also allow you to experiment with new patterns. I pair up the new dangerous and experimental model with a trusted "old dependable". For me, the pros outweigh the cons, and always will.

Dropper-Fly Attachments – Only One Good Choice

You can attach a dropper fly to your leader six different ways. First let's consider the most popular and easiest way to secure a second fly to a nymph leader. Come up about two feet from the end of the tippet where the point, or terminal, fly will be tied. Cut the leader at this point. Put the 22- – 24-inch piece of line aside for a moment. With a clinch knot tie the dropper fly onto the leader that remains. Now, the two-foot tippet remnant is tied to the bend of the hook of the dropper fly using a clinch knot. Then the point fly is tied at the very end of the leader set-up. Done.

The dropper fly can be quickly changed out for another candidate. I have used this method to secure the second fly, and I have caught fish with it. However,

I have also missed hooking too many fish which have struck at the dropper fly. Yes, there is a major drawback with this system: a fish may be startled when its nose hits the leader as it tries to intercept the fly, or its nose will push the leader which, then, pushes the fly away from the fish as it tries to bite it. Not good.

The fly hook of the dropper nymph needs to have no impediment preventing the fish from cleanly accessing the entire hook. Additionally, the fly needs to swim and wiggle naturally by hanging free of the main leader. The in-line attachment method just described does not allow this freedom. So, it is my belief that not only are more fish missed on the strike, fewer fish actually strike the fly, too. Bad combo.

The One Best Dropper Set-Up

Let's back up to the point where the lower two feet of the tippet is cut from the main leader. Now rejoin the two lines where they were cut using a double surgeon's knot. When the knot is properly tied there will be two

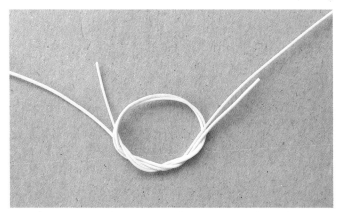

The surgeon's knot is simpler, easier, and quicker to tie than the blood knot. The dropper fly is tied on the "downstream" unclipped tag end of the knot.

short tag ends which would normally be cut off. One tag points up the leader toward the rod tip, while the other points in the direction of the point fly on the very end of the leader. In setting up my dropper-fly system, the tag end pointing to the point fly (get it?) is the one to which I will tie my dropper nymph. I purposely manipulate the tag ends as I tie the surgeon's knot so that the tag to which the fly is secured is about 4 inches long when I pull everything tight. This allows me enough length to tie on the fly with a clinch knot. The other tag end is trimmed short, of course. When the dropper fly is tied in place it should hang no more than 3 inches from the main leader. Two to three inches is the ideal range. If the dropper line is more than 3 inches it will tend to twist and foul on the leader as it is cast or fished. This, my friends, is the most effective way to create a dropper set-up. Maximizes your chances and it's your best hope for hooking and holding a fish.

So why isn't my suggested dropper system used more widely? Because it's a bit tedious compared to the most often used system mentioned above, and when the dropper is broken off, or the need arises to change the dropper fly for another, there may not be sufficient line length to tie on another fly. In this case it could involve reconstructing the lower portion of the leader in order to maintain the proper lengths and distances of the flies and split shot and strike indicator. For this reason I usually fish my most dependable nymph on the dropper, while the secondary or experimental fly which I may want to change is tied on the point. The point fly is easily and quickly changed out with a clinch knot.

A Case for Barbless Hooks

Anyone who has fished, even on an occasional basis, has a tale or two about someone in their circle – maybe themselves – who has had a penetrating encounter with a fishing hook, usually a barbed hook. And, of course, I have stories of my own which remind me of the smart advantage of using barbless hooks.

One of my most memorable was a mid-September day on the Rogue River with Chuck and Paul. It all began when Chuck, fishing in the rear of the boat, broke off a fly on a snag on the river bottom. I handed him a replacement nymph, a #12 Copper John. He tied it to his leader, but before he resumed casting Paul in the front of the boat hooked a steelhead. He wanted Chuck's help as I continued to man the oars in pursuit of the fish.

As Chuck moved toward the bow, he laid his rod horizontally along the side of the boat. In his haste the rod's perch was insecure and it began to fall toward the

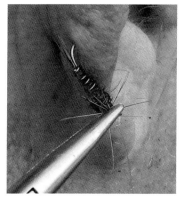
Did you hear something?

boat floor. With cat-like reflexes I grabbed the rod just above the cork grip to prevent damage to a very expensive fly reel. Simultaneously I also had grasped the new hook just tied on the leader, which stung me hard in the tip of the middle finger on my left hand. To be more precise, the hook was buried all the way up to the body of the fly! After snipping the line at the fly with my teeth I tried to forcefully back the fly out of my finger. It did not budge. With blood dripping on my waders and the cooler stationed beside me, I asked Chuck if he had removed the barb from the hook. When he replied "I thought you did!" my pulse rate increased a click.

As I have told every listener of this story, when you lock a forceps on a deeply imbedded hook to remove it, you must "swing for the fence". If you don't yank with conviction you may not get a second chance before you faint. I hit the necessary home run and the blood flow ramped up. How cool. I left a trail of red as I shortly moved forward in the boat to net Paul's steelhead. Then, it was time for lunch and clean up.

Another very important consideration for barbless hooks is the easier, usually less damaging, removal from a fish to be released. The damage done at the wound site by a barbed hook, however, is small compared to the potential fatal damage incurred by the fish when it is squeezed hard by a fisherman's hand as it struggles while being handled. A fatally injured fish may swim away after being released, but its life will soon end.

If you wish to point to a fish mortality study where barb-hooked fish were captured, the hooks removed, and very few deaths were noted, discover *who* handled and released the fish. You may discover that the fish handlers in the experiment were not 15-year-old kids with spinning rods and a box of worms. A legitimate study would have been conducted on a stream or lake with a random group of "civilian" fishermen left to their own fish-releasing devices. I suspect the mortality rate would have been significantly higher. Those who claim the use of barbed hooks does not result in many more fish deaths due to handling as the squirming slippery fish is subdued in order to dislodge them are mistaken.

As for the holding power of a barbed hook versus a barbless one, the sleeker, narrower-profile barbless hook point penetrates deeper with less hook-setting force than a larger-profile barbed hook.

Removable Split Shot

If you fish two small nymphs together there is a very good possibility there will not be adequate weight to enable the flies to sink quickly. In this case, use *removable* split shot where it is legal. Removable split shot can be difficult to locate, but it is a necessary part of the system since you will be constantly adding and removing the weights to match the changing combinations of water depth and current speed. Too little weight, the flies do not get to the bottom quickly; too much weight the flies drag along the bottom, and often snag obstructions there. To be effective and maximize the fish count, weighting adjustments are made constantly. To paraphrase an old adage: The difference between an average nymph fisherman and one who is a world-class nymphing assassin is one more (or one less) split shot.

I recommend size 'BB' shot; I may use one, or I may use five. The removability feature allows the angler to re-use the shot, without the necessity of cutting and rejoining the tippet, which is necessary for standard non-removable split shot.

A Legal Weight on the Leader

With the exception of the fly-fishing-only section of Oregon's North Umpqua River, there is nowhere in Oregon of which I am aware that does not allow the use of weighted flies. Besides the possibility of catching a fish on the fly with significant weight on or in it, it serves as a legal weight which will get a small fly down to drift near the river bottom. As to whether the weighted fly should be placed on the dropper line or on the point, I decide which fly I am most likely to change. The fly – whether big or small – most likely to be changed out is tied on the point. Most often I will tie the heavily weighted fly on the point because I will need to tie on a heavier or lighter fly throughout my fishing day. With any given weighted fly pattern I will have tied them in a variety of sizes, so just as with the split shot, I can fine-tune the amount of weight needed to match any given combination of current speed and depth.

Strike Indicators

There are many different choices for strike indicators: materials, designs, colors, and sizes. For many years I used synthetic yarn which I shaped into something resembling a carnation. When floating high these were highly visible and very sensitive in detecting the strike. However, they

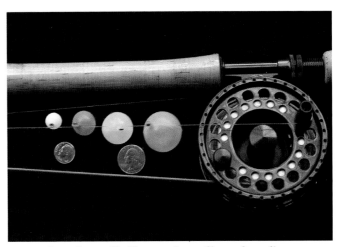

A variety of indicator sizes allows for adjustments for the river's turbulence, the weight of the flies, and the eyesight acuity of the angler.

tended to get water logged and needed constant combing and fly-floatant application. With the advent of soft plastic bubble indicators available in four different sizes, I have transitioned to these exclusively for nymphing moving water. They come in some highly visible colors, and they always float, as long as a hook point does not find them. The size I find most useful is about the diameter of a quarter.

The soft bubble indicator has a small metal grommet on it so a loop of line can be threaded through it and, then, looped over the bubble and pulled tight. To move the indicator up or down the leader the process is reversed, and re-secured at its new location.

A couple of problems arise from the bubble's design. One, the bubble may slide down the leader toward the flies when the cast is forceful. If attention is not paid to this possibility, the indicator may not have adequate distance from the flies to allow the nymphs to reach the river bottom.

The second problem arises with the leader zone where the grommet contacts the line. It's very distressing when a big fish is hooked and the leader breaks where the grommet has worn through the line. Not only is the fish lost, but so is the entire business end of the leader as it detaches from the indicator. And, there's no guarantee the drifting indicator can be apprehended before floating around the next bend in the river.

Though you will give up some fine-tuning possibilities, remedy both of these problems by inserting a couple of snap swivels 15 – 18 inches apart on the upper leader. The indicator is locked in place and cannot wear on the line. I have experimented with letting the bubble slide freely on the line between the two swivels.

Multiple rods allow for using different flies and a variety of leader lengths with no set-up time needed, which translates into more fishing time.

My only concern is that, because the indicator is not firmly attached, subtle strikes may go undetected as the leader slips softly through the grommet hole without adequately affecting the drift of the bubble to signal a strike. I continue to experiment with three swivels on the leader about 15 inches apart. I am not yet convinced it's necessary. With two swivels I want to make sure that I position them with a little extra distance, whereby the distance between the indicator and nymphs is a bit too long, and never too short.

Multiple Rods

A time-saving strategy is to have multiple nymph rods set up at all times. I have a rod set up for "shallow" water situations with water depths of 3 to 5 feet and a second rod with a longer leader to fish depths over 5 feet. In addition to precisely fishing a broad range of depths with minimal changes necessary, I can have different nymphs on each rod. Multiple rods also mean more fishing time. With two anglers, I often have three nymph rods set up. If the flies are lost to the bottom or a big fish, a tangle occurs, or I want to have them try different flies, the angler can use the third nymph rod.

Overcoming Inertia

M. Scott Peck, in his classic work *The Road Less Traveled*, maintains that what we all share as humans is a tendency towards laziness. For the sake of delicate egos, including my own, I will refer to this inclination in us as *inertia*. In physics, inertia is the state where a body (me) at rest tends to stay at rest until acted upon by a force. As this applies to nymph fishing, there are many little details that need to be attended at any time — leader length, indicator adjustments, fly changes, and constantly monitoring the correct amount of weight needed for an effective drift of the nymphs. It's one thing to know what needs to be done to maximize the fish catch with nymphing methods; it's another to diligently implement the details, to overcome our inertia, and take the fly-fishing road less traveled. This proactive diligence about tending the details is a key contributor to consistently effective nymphing. It is not a game for those with chronic inertia . . . or inclined to laziness.

FIVE

Locating River Trout and Steelhead

D epending on the species, trout in rivers and streams may be found to prefer different water types. Though a given piece of moving water may simultaneously hold a variety of species, often there is some segregation which has naturally evolved so that all are not competing for the same foods, same habitat, and same spawning locations. It is quite natural that survival for all species is best when they do not live in a single crowded neighborhood.

Steelhead are sea-going rainbow trout, so when I discuss locating one I am also discussing locating the other. Their habits and preferences are essentially the same. As they approach spawning time, once-bright steelhead return to their original rainbow trout color scheme and can be easily mistaken for huge resident rainbows.

We must begin by considering the three different combinations of fish and their particular environments: trout in rivers, trout and other popular game fish in lakes and ponds, and steelhead in rivers. Each combination is different, each with its own peculiarities and set of unique challenges.

What All Fish Share in Common

Fish are cold-blooded. This means their body temperature matches the water temperature. Like us, all fish have a preferred temperature range where they are most comfortable and most active. The more active the fish, the more calories it burn. The more cals burned, the more food needed to replenish the store of energy. Knowing the preferred temperature range of the particular fish you want to catch is important information. Often it's an important predictor of your success. It matters little how good your equipment, flies, and technique if the water temperature is 38 degrees Fahrenheit and you are targeting rainbow or brown trout. They don't need to feed much because their metabolism and calorie consumption is very low. The odds of success are usually slim. The same is true if you attempt to catch brook trout when the water temperature is 75 degrees. Just as the water temperature can be too cold for much fishing action, it can also be too warm.

Here are some very generalized temperature ranges for some of the most sought after freshwater species in both moving and stillwaters.

Brown trout: 50 – 74 degrees Fahrenheit
Rainbow trout: 42 – 62
Steelhead: 38 – 62
Cutthroat: 48 – 65
Brook trout (a char): 44 – 65
Kokanee (landlocked salmon): 50 – 60
Largemouth bass: 50 – 80
Crappie and bluegill: 58 – 75

Don't get bogged down in the details here. The thermal guidelines above are a compilation of many "experts". As you will quickly notice, virtually all the fish above — and some I did not mention — will be happily active when the water temperature is 50 – 60 degrees. Within reason, these fish can all be caught a bit above or below their preferred ranges. What I am trying to convey is that an angler new to nymphing may have selected the right flies and equipment, and have adequate skills, but may find the fish unwilling to bite. The angler may mistakenly think he and his gear are to blame when actually the water is too warm or too cold. It is quite natural after a long winter to go to the river

Small streams are great places to learn about locating fish and fine-tuning nymphing skills. Many have an array of different structure and holding water types.

or lake after a few days of nice weather in late winter or early spring. The air temperature can be quite pleasant but the water temperature can remain stubbornly cold. When it comes to trout fishing, I definitely will choose a lake or pond over a river if I need to catch maximum numbers.

Another environmental factor that can throw river fish off the bite is a sudden rise in the water level. In addition to dropping the water temperature a few degrees, which the fish usually do not like, the increased flow will often cause the river to muddy. A snowmelt during a few warm days in the spring, or heavy rain, can cool and muddy a river. It may take the fish a few days, or longer, to adjust to the changed river conditions before they resume a more normal eating routine.

Trout in Streams:
An Excellent Nymphing Starting Point

If an angler new to nymph fishing would ask me where to start, where to begin to learn the basics of nymph fishing, I would tell them to seek out a quality trout stream. Two reasons: trout are abundant and they are always in search of something to eat. A small one is best in order to view and easily cover multiple fish-holding water types in microcosm fashion. If it's a freestone stream with riffles and rapids, runs, and pools, with an abundance of boulders, the fish will usually be easy to locate once the angler knows how to "read' the water. Here in the western U.S. there is a magnificent abundance of such rivers and streams.

Fishing flat-water portions of rivers and streams is much like fishing a lake. Stealth and a breeze are quite helpful.

If the river is of low gradient with a flat, uniform surface, locating the fish will be more challenging if they are not feeding on the surface or observed cruising in clear water. It usually takes time and experience to read flat expanses of moving waters. The underwater

structure — pockets, transition zones, weed beds, drop-offs, significant boulders, channels and ledges — must be discovered. This is best accomplished by walking a smaller river, or floating others where possible, with a high sun and polarized glasses to see and understand zones where fish will congregate. Slower, flat-surface rivers are best approached as if searching for fish in a lake, which will be discussed in a future chapter.

So, what now follows is most applicable to freestone rivers, but most of the same fish-holding water types also apply to flat-water rivers. It's just that the features can be somewhat muted, not as easily observed for the beginner or foreigner to flat water.

Pockets

Assuming I have a myriad of water type options for introducing a novice on the basics of effective nymphing, I would choose to fish pocket water for a variety of reasons. First, pockets are usually small expanses, easily covered with a succession of short casts, and line control for an effective drift or swing is easy with following simple instructions. Secondly, the water surrounding pockets is quite busy, choppy, "loud". An angler's presence is obscured to some degree, so the fish are not easily alarmed if reasonable stealth is employed. Thirdly, by the nature of the water in which they hold, pocket fish are often willing and aggressive biters.

What exactly is "pocket" water? They are small fish-holding locations usually associated with swift water and structure. In a boulder-strewn rapid are found areas of quieter (not dead still) water in front of, behind, or beside large rocks. If a boulder is submerged, the pocket immediately downstream of it may be fishable. If the rock is exposed above the river's surface, the pocket behind it may have slack "dead" water or an eddy that does not hold fish, or makes it impossible to present a nymph in a convincing manner. Commonly, there is the notion that the pocket immediately behind a boulder is always a good fishing-holding spot. I'm very discriminating in seeking zones with a uni-directional current, not a swirling eddy. Fish may hold in the eddy but nymphing them effectively is difficult, rarely worth the time unless the eddy is large. In such cases, find a uni-directional current within the eddy, where you *can* fish it effectively.

When nymph fishing salmon that often prefer holding in eddies, large eddies are much easier to fish effectively than tiny swirly pockets.

Though most pockets are associated with a rapid, there are solitary steelhead pockets near a solitary

On a larger river with limited access a pontoon boat can get an angler to fish others cannot reach.
A small boat can traverse shallow waters where a larger drift boat cannot safely go.

boulder or a scour in the stream bottom where the river's currents have carved out an obvious deeper water depression surrounded entirely by shallower water. These are like little oases in the desert. A migrating steelhead may have traveled a considerable distance through unsuitable holding water when it finally happens upon a pocket where a pause is in order.

Depending on the specific characteristics of a pocket, nymphs will catch fish. Because they are usually small, pockets do not take long to cover. I fish them thoroughly and quickly; then, move on. Pocket-holding fish, if interested at all, will usually reveal themselves quickly. I have a "hit and run" mindset. The more pockets I can fish, the more fish I will catch for the day.

Tailouts

Think of sprinting uphill . . . against the wind. Just like a fatigued runner, migrating or restless fish coursing their way upstream against the swift currents of a rapid will be inclined to rest a bit once they have reached quiet water.

The smooth, tamer water immediately upstream of a rapid is a tailout. Using round numbers, the tailout may extend from ten to fifty feet upstream of a rapid. Though no two are exactly alike, the typical tailout will range from a few inches to two to four feet deep across its breadth, from bank to bank. Factoring in the combination of current velocity, depth, and stream-bottom structure, a steelhead or traveling trout may linger just above the rapid for a while if left undisturbed. Because the typical tailout has flat, unriffled surface currents, and is rather shallow, the fish can be exposed. Observant predators and anglers will be able to locate a fish parked in a tailout. You can bet experienced, larger fish will be on high alert for danger. A larger individual has not survived to this point in its life by being careless. Therefore, stealth is of extreme importance to the would-be successful nymph angler.

The two best options for the fly-fisherman (especially a steelheader) in the typical tailout are the skated dry fly and the swinging wet fly. Not nymphs. But if a particular tailout is not much more than a walking-pace

Joann Severson is all smiles on a winter day fishing an egg fly under an indicator, using the dead-drift nymphing method.

velocity, preferably riffled, and is at least three feet deep, both swinging and dead-drift nymphs can entice the fish.

I have a favorite tailout on Oregon's Rogue River where there is a deep depression at the lower end of it where steelhead often hold, after having just negotiated the speeding water of a heavy rapids. They move into this pocket to sit protected from the quick water passing over them. My clients and I have caught scores of steelhead and trout over the years with wet flies. When the sun is high, the best approach is to nymph this spot. My angling ace sister, Joann, hooked three steelhead one March day dead-drifting egg flies into the depression in this tailout.

Runs

A run, by my definition, is a wide and long expanse of river where the aggregate of current velocity, depth and structure is abundant throughout. Submerged boulders are often plentiful in such areas. The trout and steelhead are happy to rest just about anywhere in a good run, so you must very systematically cover the this type of prime water throughout its entire width and length, though there may be a few special boulders or pockets within the run that are especially attractive to traveling steelhead. Think of these as the best "homes' in an excellent neighborhood.

Where the run is three to ten feet deep, nymph fishing can be deadly. Let's review for just a moment systematically covering the likely fish-holding water of a run.

Cast the fly upstream, roughly at an angle of 45 – 60 degrees from straight across the river's current, allowing the flies to sink on a slack line. Most of the slack — but not all — is gathered as it drifts back with the current. If a fish intercepts the fly, the line will hesitate

or tighten. At this point you may not feel the strike, only visually detect it. Since an artificial fly has no agreeable taste, smell or texture, the steelhead holds it only briefly before expelling it. From interception to expulsion may be a second or less. This is a game of quick draw. You must be alert and respond quickly to have any hope of hooking the fish. A strike indicator serves as an invaluable visual aid in detecting a grab.

An additional fly-fishing method you can employ in covering a run for steelhead involves the use of my Hybrid Line System, which I discuss on page 127. Using interchangeable sinking-tips attached to a running line, I cast the rig upstream at approximately a 45-degree angle, just as I do when fishing a floating line and indicator. Let the fly to sink on a slack line. The nymphing method is employed during the drift until the system is approximately 45 degrees downstream of your position. Then, after the line is mended upstream of the fly, it arcs across the current on a tight line, fishing the nymph or egg under tension. You will definitely feel the strike. Two nymphing methods — dead-drift and tight-line swing — are employed on the same drift of the flies.

Runs take time to methodically cover properly. Most have a "sweet spot" which is a dependable fish-holding zone season after season. Think treasure hunt when fishing a run.

Channels

A channel is a well-defined narrow band of deep water bounded by shallow water or ledge rock. These are often found near the river's edge, close to the bank. I refer to them as "dark green highways". Where a run is relatively broad, a channel is much narrower by comparison. Channels are havens for resting and nymph-feeding trout, and literally used as highways for traveling steelhead. Where the fish find depth, cover, and suitable structure in the

Think of a channel as a highway where fish travel. Especially at lower water, channels are quite obvious and worth covering thoroughly, particularly those zones replete with large, submerged boulders.

course of a channel, they are prompted to linger. As always, make sure to very systematically cover all the water in a channel.

As I write this section, I have just finished with my four-month Rogue River guiding season. During my last week the two most dependable fish-catching locations on a nine-mile stretch of river were channels. These narrow bands of fishy water put the trout and steelhead in very defined, observable locations.

As a fly-fishing guide, a drift boat is my vehicle of choice to get my clients to productive holding water. A whitewater boat ride adds to the day's fun.

Anchor your boat to the side of a channel, at a reasonable casting distance, but far enough away that you won't alarm the fish. Starting at the top of the channel, make sure its entire width is covered with effective drifts of the flies. Then pull the anchor, drop down a boat length or two, and begin the casting routine over again, until the entire length of the channel has been covered. If on foot, and the channel is approachable by casting from the bank or by wading, the same routine applies except that you may start at the lower terminus of the channel and work your way upstream, approaching the fish from behind, since they are facing upstream.

Ledges

Think of a channel with just one very abrupt side. Fish will rest near or travel along a ledge — a vertical or near-vertical drop-off, a rocky shelf. If the depth is adequate, at least three feet, and the flow velocity is reasonable, there's a chance the water near a ledge can hold fish.

Most ledges have a Sweet Spot. There is something peculiar about the structure and hydraulics in a precise location which causes a fish to hold in this small zone along the ledge. Make sure the Sweet Spot is thoroughly covered with effective drifts of the nymphs before moving on. With clients I have to coach them about casting

It's always great to catch a trout on a dry fly, but most of the time they are focused on subsurface dining fare. This Colorado brown trout ate a San Juan Plus, one of my all-star flies.

Holding along ledges, fish have a sense of security. Fishing zones next to ledges are narrow, usually no more than a rod length wide, so they can be quickly and accurately covered.

distance, angle of the cast, mending, and good rod tip position through the entirety of the drift.

Ledge-water productivity can be temperamental. Each has its optimal water level. As the height of the river fluctuates up and down, deviating from the optimal range, the fish will hold elsewhere. When I explore a ledgy area on a new river to which I am committed to learning well, and fail to catch fish there, I want to fish it at a variety of river levels to discover the optimal combination of flow and depth for holding biting trout or steelhead.

Cut Banks

For rivers and streams with undercut banks, trout and other predators may very well take up residence in these recesses. They have all a trout can want: comfort, protection, and a prime location to wait for food that drifts or swims by. Big brown trout, in particular, love undercuts.

Casting from mid river to the bank is a good approach if the situation permits. But often I enjoy the challenge of quietly walking on the bank casting a significant distance either up- or downstream from my position. When fishing nymphs I always prefer to work upstream, approaching the fish from behind.

Stealth is of utmost concern. The vibration of careless footsteps will put fish which lurk in undercuts on high alert. Additionally, when a fish leaves its lair to turn downstream in pursuit of your nymphs it may see you as you stand waiting to set the hook. To minimize discovery of your presence, fish quietly on your knees if the bank and its terrain allow it.

Channels and Depressions in Stream-Bottom Vegetation

Some rivers have an abundance of vegetation, in which crustaceans and insects thrive. Trout will forage in and around the plants, and have nearby safe havens to hide in and under should threats arrive. Because plants thrive in sunlight, many streams with regions of "weed beds" are shallow and the surface currents are flat, not riffled, stealth is of utmost importance. Longer, lighter leaders, tiny indicators, lightly-weighted nymphs and long casts are usually required. Because current velocities are usually slower in these low-gradient vegetation zones, I may use a float tube, as if I am fishing a slow-moving lake. Idaho's famous Silver Creek has portions which lend themselves to this approach.

Seams

A seam is the boundary between fast water and slow water. Seams can range from a couple of feet to a couple of rod lengths wide. This is a transition zone where the water may be to the liking of a resting fish. The swift current on one side of the seam is too fast for a fish to hold comfortably. The slower moving, or slack water, on the other side of the seam can be too quiet to be attractive or secure for the trout or steelhead, so they travel and hold along the seam.

Walk slowly and softly while fishing cut banks. Heavy footsteps and a high standing position can alert bank-hugging fish. How can you spot an effective cut-bank angler? Grass-stained knees.

Use both the dead-drift and swinging nymphing methods to fish seams. A natural drift of the flies is best, but it's always worth the time casting nymphs into the faster water, then, swing them into and across the seam. Start at the upstream end of the target area and systematically work your way downstream until you have covered its entire length.

Fish holding in graveled lanes and expanses in heavily vegetated streams can often be sighted before fishing to them. My choice is a lightly weighted nymph, no additional weight, and no indicator, especially to fish I can see. If the fish moves as my fly approaches I assume it is intercepting my nymph.

When probing the water with the dead-drift method, start at either the upstream or downstream terminus of the productive water, working until you have covered the entire length of the seam. Drop the nymphs into the seam and allow them to drift naturally with the current through the heart of the prime water.

Transition Zones

There are obvious fish-holding zones where shallow-water areas transition into deeper water. The river bottom slopes downward from being too shallow to hold fish into deeper, prime-fishing water of three to seven feet in depth, but I may lengthen my leader and fish into ten feet of water in certain areas that I know are holding fish.

A transition can work the opposite way, too: water that may be too deep to fish effectively with a fly starts to "shallow up" at its downstream end. A pool or run that may be ten to twenty feet deep will eventually transition into the reasonable depth range.

When I'm fishing steelhead in the summer and fall, I'm always nymphing, or my clients are, when sun is on the fish-holding water.

In the cold water of winter and early spring I am nymphing exclusively with egg or shrimp-like flies, using a floating line and indicator. To seek out steelhead that prefer a different presentation of the fly, I go

Sometimes seams can only be fished from directly upstream, swimming and swinging the nymphs slowly downstream. In can be effective to twitch or pulse these flies.

through a second time with the Hybrid Line System, and same flies. The Hybrid Line keeps flies deeper during the tight-line swing of the egg and shrimp flies.

Areas in a river where currents flow from the shallows into deeper runs and pools are obvious good nymphing zones, assuming the water is not too fast. Working upstream from behind the fish is always a good strategy.

There are fish-holding locations that do not easily fall into any one single water-type category as described here. Rather than worrying about how to categorize a specific water that might hold a willing fish, try to discern if the water in front of you has the characteristics that would encourage a fish to hold there: current velocity, depth and structure. Match the nymphing details to the light and river conditions, the structural nature of the chosen piece of water, you skills, and the nymphing methods and equipment you enjoy using.

Pools

Pools are obvious fish-holding locations. Pools can be large or small; wide or narrow; have fast currents, or slow; be monstrously deep, or only moderately so. But, they all have three portions in common: a transition zone at the head, a deep 'heart', and a tailout. Since identifying and fishing tailouts and transition zones has already been addressed, let's focus on fishing the heart of the pool.

As you assess the potential of hooking a good trout or steelhead in a pool, take into consideration the current velocity, depth and structure of the piece of water,

From a high vantage point an angler may be able to sight fish holding in the depths of a pool. Neutral clothing colors and minimal casting movements enhance the possibility of success.

as usual. The very first thing I study is the direction and evenness of the current. Swirling, multi-directional currents are difficult to fish effectively. The direction of the fly drift is unpredictable, and not only do you have a wacky horizontal drift of the hook, there may be an up-and-down swimming component as the fly moves as well. You want a straight-line, uni-directional drift where you are in contact with what is happening. Strikes are often soft, subtle, a quiet interception. There is very little time to sense the take and set the hook, if it is even seen at all. Unless I can actually see a fish in swirly water in a pool, I bypass it to focus on those portions of the pool with a uniform current.

The depth of any given pool can vary greatly: degrees of shallow along its periphery, and deep to very deep in the heart. I may adjust the nymphing method, leader length, and flies as I fish the shallower edges, then the deep center. Think of breaking the central portion of the pool into smaller parts. Each part is a fishing entity unto itself. If the current and conditions are right, fish the shallower edges (3 – 7 feet) with minimal adjustments. Direct sunlight or shade, broken water or smooth surface, and limitations on fishing position as you make the cast will all affect the fine-tuning changes you must make.

Adjustments in leader length and indicator location are necessary in deep water. You may have to lengthen your 9- – 10-foot leader to 15. The easiest way to do so is

by adding more tippet with a double surgeon's knot. A 13-foot two-hand rod makes fishing a very long leader a much easier proposition than the commonly used nine-footer. If the water is more than 10 feet deep, I may remove the indicator and focus on the movement of the floating fly line. Because of the great distance from the water's surface to the river bottom there is usually a large disparity in water velocities from top to bottom. A leader without an indicator, especially if there is a little upwelling and down-welling of the current, seems to get a truer, more natural drift. Since the detection of the strike is lessened without an indicator, I set the hook more often, at the slightest hint of a hesitation in the line or leader. I am always pleasantly surprised when I come tight against a fish when I fancied the small hesitation in the drift could not possibly have been a strike. Again, there are no penalty points for setting the hook, so look for any excuse to do so. This type of situation is also tailor-made for the Hybrid Line. This line system excels in deeper water.

If the current in the heart of the pool is slower than a walking speed, I may scale down the tippet diameter and tie on a smaller fly. A suspicious trout or steelhead has a longer time to study the fly and detect the leader tied to it. Smaller and lighter is less threatening, more apt to result in a hookup. Other anglers may ignore slower currents, or they may fail to scale back their terminal gear. These oversights can offer you someone else's overlooked opportunity.

Pools are prime candidates for holding resting fish, top, middle and bottom. I remind myself to be particularly patient, and willing to change-up the method and flies to fish the heart of the pools. When the sun is high, and there is a lot of human activity on the river, the deepest heart of the pool offers maximum protection for wary fish. The first requisite for effective nymph fishing is to focus angling time where fish are actually holding. Pools hold willing fish for those who rise to the challenge.

Special Boulders: Fish Magnets

I have a special fishing spot christened Magic Rock, named by my good fishing friend Chuck Wagner. The moniker is appropriate. When the river flows are anything except quite low in early fall a biting steelhead can be dependably found near Magic Rock. Every river has this type of special spot — where the right combination of hydraulics and depth draws the fish like a magnet. Some of these stones are exposed partially above the surface at certain flows, but the best ones, the most reliable ones, are those that are fully submerged, like Magic Rock.

Fish are drawn to underwater structure that offers them both protection from fatiguing currents and predators. They may also be attracted to structure that serves as good habitat for insects and crustaceans which they can eat.

Fish-attracting boulders are often found by accident. If clients or I hook trout or steelhead in a piece of water I am careful to note exactly our location. I am motivated on multiple levels to remember where to place the flies the next time I'm fishing this particular place.

Virtually All Water Types are Hybrids

The vast majority of quality holding water zones that can't be categorized as solely one type or another are hybrids of multiple water types. They are mixes. I find it helpful to break up complicated, hybrid pieces of river into smaller, digestible chunks. This is particularly important to beginners who might be overwhelmed as they survey a piece of water. Work on one portion at a time. The exceptional nympher will make the necessary adjustments in the leader, flies, weight, casting, mending, and position. Think small, study, experiment, adjust, and conquer.

SIX

Stream-Trout All-Star Nymphs

The **Gold Ribbed Hare's Ear**, and its variations, such as my favored Flashback pattern pictured here, is the second nymph to make all my All-Star teams. Originating in the mid 1800's this nymph has stood the test of time like no other. The spiky guard hairs in the fur trap and hold gas bubbles on the body of the fly. This simulates what some hatching insects do in the real world. Fish recognize this and mistake the Hare's Ear for real food. Excellent ruse.

The nymphs, larvae, and pupae All-Stars shown here are flies I am confident will catch trout in streams and rivers anywhere on the globe — New Zealand, Argentina, Ireland, Canada, and my "home" streams in the western USA. Since I fish larval imitations and many pupae using various nymphing methods, I have grouped them with standard nymph patterns. In addition to stream- and season-specific patterns, these All-Stars will always be found in my fishing vest every day I'm on the river.

The **Prince** is the captain of my stream-fishing All-Star Team. It is one of only two nymphs listed on all teams — stream trout, stillwater trout, and steelhead. The peacock body paired with white biots is an irresistible combination for trout and steelhead. Fished in sizes 10 – 16, with or without a metal bead at the head, this is my Number One go-to nymph in trout streams.

In many freestone streams and rivers stonefly nymphs abound. Larger species have a three-year life cycle, which means even after the oldest generation has hatched for the year, generations 2 and 3 are in the river living their daily lives among the rocks and rubble of the stream bottom . . . and perpetually available to be eaten by trout. My neutrally-colored **Gorman Golden Stonefly Nymph** in sizes 6 – 10 was my second best all-time selling nymph during my fly shop retails days. Yes, the Prince was tops.

The **Copper John** swept into the trout fly-fishing world in the late 1990's. It's been a nymphing monster. I consider it the best nymph pattern of its generation. The shiny copper wire body gets a fish's attention. And, it can be tied in many different wire colors other than the standard copper to approximate insects of particular interest — green, red, blue, black, chartreuse, yellow, silver, wine, and spiraled color combinations. Sizes 12 – 18.

Ring-necked pheasant tail fibers are hairy and buggy. The **Pheasant Tail Nymph** does a superb job of simulating living aquatic insects with bodies with fine hairs on them. Many effective nymph, larvae, and pupal fly patterns utilize pheasant tail. There are some very worthy variations of this fly which can be tied with or without a metal bead at the head, beads of various finishes, and strips of pearlescent mylar over the body and/ or thorax can sometimes add to its effectiveness. Sizes 12 – 18. Tiny size 16 and 18 beadless models are excellent Chironomid pupa imitations.

The **Bead Head Serendipity** has its roots on Montana's Madison River. The original did not have a bead and was known as the RAM Caddis, for its creator Ross A. Marigold. I'm sure I was not the first to tie it with a bead, but I definitely prefer this larva/pupa pattern with a silver bead. The synthetic Antron body has an affinity for gas bubbles just like spiky hare's fur does. Olive,

brown, tan, chartreuse, wine, and black are my favorite colors. Sizes 12 – 18.

Dan Delekta's **Mega Prince** is a fish-catcher. Inspired by the original Prince Nymph, this is a larger, more elaborate rendition. The lively and buggy body materials, with the addition of rubber legs, is a very passable stonefly nymph imitation. There are times when the trout respond readily when this nymph is swung and twitched at the conclusion of its drift. Sizes 6 – 10 work best for me.

Especially in slightly muddy stream flows the **San Juan Worm** is a killer fly. To spice it up, to add some eye-catching glitz that trout seem to like, I add three or four strands of red Krystal Flash fore and aft on the fly. My friend Rick Rossi, a superb Montana fly-fishing guide, uses the Worm anywhere, anytime, and all the time. And, they are easy and fast to tie. Red is the standard, but dirty pink, tan, and wine are popular colors, too. Sizes 6 – 12.

It's built like a wet fly but I fish it like a nymph. When caddisflies and mayflies are hatching, the **Bird's Nest** is an excellent nymph to fish both dead-drift on the first portion of the nymphing presentation, and particularly deadly as the line comes tight to swing up and across. I find little slow twitches during the swing can be the trigger for reluctant fish. Olive and dark brown are excellent color choices, in addition to medium brown. Can be tied with a bead, too. Sizes 12 – 16.

This versatile caddis of my own creation fishes well as both a caddis larva and pupa, and performs on both the dead-drift and the swing. The **Skinny Minnie Caddis** design has the lure of peacock, mottled partridge wing case and beard, and two little sexy strands of pearl Krystal Flash on the underside. Sizes 10 – 16.

When I need a particularly nasty stonefly nymph on heavily fished rivers I bust out the turbo-charged version of my GG Stonefly, the **GG Scorpion**. It's a pain to tie, and I'm always tempted to swim the rapids or chop down a tree to rescue it, but "this dog can hunt." Since I have to tie this tedious hell hound myself, I'm most inclined not to share it with others who might not appreciate it as much as I do. Sizes 6 and 8.

The **Posse Bugger** has a burley pupa design. It doesn't look like anything special but the fish think otherwise. Stream trout think so much of it that it's one of my All-Stars. Even with its Plain Jane appearance, this fly is one of my favorite swinging nymphs. Part of the "secret" I think is the two strands of flat pearlescent mylar in the tail. The Posse is particularly deadly in the mid Willamette Valley streams where I live in northwestern Oregon. Sizes 10 – 14.

SEVEN

The Nuances of Nymphing Effectively in Rivers

Josh Cuperus, master nympher.

I t's time to catch a fish! Once the gear, leader, flies, fishing location, and river conditions are all as they should be, the moment has arrived to put the nymph in front of a fish and convince the trout or steelhead to eat it. Keep in mind that what follows is applicable to both trout and steelhead, since a steelhead is a sea-going rainbow *trout*. Here's how I do it.

I survey the expanse of river I have chosen to determine where the fish will be holding. Because fish face into the current, I want to station myself at the downstream end of the likely water, so I approach the fish from behind them. They are looking away from me. Assuming I am fishing on foot, if I move quietly and slowly I can get close enough to make casts of reasonable length to reach them. Casts within 40 feet (think 4 – 5 rod lengths) allow for accuracy, line control, and strike detection.

When fishing from a boat I cannot always begin covering a stretch of water from the downstream end first. The current may be too strong to start low and work upstream. If the water is not too deep, I may actually get out of my boat and slowly walk it upstream as my clients cast over the water.

Mad Casting Skills on Display

Some of my experienced fly-angling clients have excellent casting skills. This can be a problem. Some with mad casting ability insist on making long casts. The problem

Roll casting is a useful skill, especially in close quarters. A standard aerialized cast with heavy nymphs and/or split on the leader can find nearby trees or an angler's face.

arises when I position the drift boat as close as possible to the holding fish so less experienced or beginner clients can easily reach the fish with relatively short casts. I have to cater to the lowest common denominator so both anglers have the opportunity to catch fish. There is something in the psyche of a few excellent fly-casters whereby they MUST cast long at all times. In spite of my instructions, and in spite of the fact that their lesser skilled fishing companion is catching fish left and right, I am unable to de-program the casting athlete. A story will illustrate . . .

A few years ago I had a man and woman team from the American Southwest join me for two days of steelhead fishing on the Rogue River. River conditions were very good and there were reasonable numbers of fish in the river. Having fished for many years at a variety of destinations around the world, he had top-quality equipment and excellent casting skills. The lady, on the other hand, had never held a fly rod before this trip. Can you see what's coming?

Whenever we approached a likely looking steelhead holding zone, I always positioned the boat as close as possible to the Red Zone without spooking the fish, usually within 35 feet of the target. One of the things I cherish about beginners, especially women, is that they tend to follow my directions and are open to learning. And, beginners have the advantage of no ingrained bad fly-fishing habits.

So for two days, when I told the lady exactly where to cast, she did it. When I suggested she mend the fly line, she did it. When the strikes came she responded as I had instructed. Once the steelhead was on the hook, she listened to and followed my coaching until the fish was in the net and the photos were taken.

Her fishing companion did not fare as well. He was in love with the long cast . . . and the steelhead were not. Though he did land two steelhead in two days, she landed seven (!) of "the fish of ten thousand casts".

To illustrate what an accomplishment this is, it took me seven years of trial-and-error effort to land my first steelhead. Granted, I had no mentor to help me along my steelhead fishing path, but what this lady did to catch challenging fish which are not large in number per river mile, and which do not have an appetite, is incredible.

This is not an unusual story. A half dozen times each guiding year, I see this same story play out. A girlfriend or spouse with no experience out-fishes her skilled boyfriend or husband. I often hear the remark, "She's always lucky", but it is not purely luck. Women have realistic expectations of success, they are relaxed, and they willingly follow directions very well. As a result, I do my best to maximize their fish-catching opportunities. I have hundreds of photos of women guests holding their prizes.

Serena Severson with a nymph-caught summer steelhead.

Though my personal attempts at re-programming long casters and the obstinate "expert" often fail, many do respond to observing their fishing partner land another fish, and another fish, and another. Especially if pride is involved, some long-distance casters eventually learn to cast as they *need* to, not to the far-away target, but to the proper target.

First Cast to Last

To maximize your chances of discovering a willing fish, cover the entire stretch of likely water very methodically. The near water is first. If I make an accurate, angled-upstream (45 - 60 degrees) cast and get what I think is a good presentation of the flies, I lengthen my line by about two feet, and reach a little bit farther for the next cast. My standing position does not change until I have covered all the water I can comfortably reach from my station. Then, I move upstream about a rod length and begin the routine again, short cast first. If you made a

plot of my standing stations, casts, and drifts of the flies, it would be a grid of overlapping arcs. Any fish in this expanse of water should have at least one chance to intercept one.

For years I made two identical casts before lengthening my line for the next two identical casts. My thinking was that perhaps the first cast may only serve to get a fish's attention, and then the second drift would be the one which the fish would strike. Interestingly, if my first cast and drift were right, I rarely caught a fish on the second cast and drift. So, what I learned was that I was reducing my effective fishing time by 50%! It was taking me twice as long to cover a piece of water because I duplicated my casts. If a fish is willing to bite a fly it is my experience it will do so the first time you make a good presentation of the fly.

Linger Longer or Leave?

One of the most critical fishing decisions you can make is how long to linger. Once the likely water has been precisely covered, it's time to move on. The odds are much greater for catching more fish if you move to a new zone where the fish are undisturbed and hungry. This is a much better strategy than continuing to pound water already fished, hoping the trout or steelhead which would not bite will miraculously change their minds.

Staying put in one spot can pay off if migrating steelhead are on the move. If it takes a long time — an hour or more — to cover a piece of water, or you have a long lunch break, it may be worth it to fish the same water a second time for new fish that may have moved in, or a fish that was alerted to you the first time through has

A "river taxi" takes hopeful anglers to the fish. Most fly-fishing guides are skilled whitewater boatmen, too. Yes, there are also skilled boatwomen.

settled down and is now willing to bite. If I decide to linger longer, I may want to cover the stretch more quickly the second time. Typically, I focus the fishing efforts on the specific Red Zone location I have mapped in the run. I lovingly refer to this as "stabbing it in the heart" before moving on to our next fishing spot.

This assumes there is another spot to fish. My typical guiding day runs just over eight hours. What this means is that I must have twenty to thirty locations to thoroughly fish with my clients. If I have only ten, we will run out of water before we run out of fishing time. So I must plan accordingly, boating an adequately long section of river to make sure there are enough fishing spots to fill the day.

It behooves any angler, whether on foot or in a boat, to know of many locations to fish in a day. Exploration time is absolutely necessary to discover quality fishing spots on a river. Plan A, B, C, D, etc. When fishing conditions are good it is not unusual to find another angler or boater occupying the water I want to fish. Rather than rudely invading someone's personal fishing space, I will move to another location. An exception to this would be is if I perceive the angler has ineffective fishing skills and appears to be almost finished with this piece of water. Waiting for the angler to vacate is a bit of a gamble. Some fishermen will stubbornly delay their departure merely to thwart my efforts to fish the water they have covered. If the situation is right I may engage in a little chess playing. My move is to drift or wade below a fisherman who does not want to move until I am gone. If he vacates the area I may be able to wade, or pull my boat, up the river to fish the spot.

Nymphing Prime Directive #1

Understanding the endpoint, knowing what is to be accomplished, is the beginning of knowing *how* to arrive at that point. Understanding where the nymph must be and what it must do (or not do) to entice the fish is the beginning of effective nymph fishing.

Though there are multiple ways to fish a nymph in rivers, I will detail the single most effective method, the one I employ 90% of the time — the dead-drift or "natural" presentation of the fly. Here's my two-part prime directive with this technique: 1) Get the nymphs into the fish's visual zone, near its holding position, not too far from eye level, a foot or two off the stream bottom. 2) The flies should drift at a speed very similar to everything else — wood and leaf debris, and drifting insects — in the trout or steelhead's immediate environment. Fish may be alarmed by anything which deviates from

this common drift speed. This holds true, also, for flies that drift too slowly, or hold stationary in the current.

With this objective clearly in mind — a natural drift of the nymphs directly in the fish's visual zone — it is necessary to know what challenges need to be met to accomplish getting a fish on the end of the line. This goal is not as easily accomplished as might be guessed.

Current Velocity with Depth

If measurements of current speeds with descent through the water column — from the surface to the river bottom — were plotted it will be seen that the fastest water is virtually at the surface and slowest near the bottom. If the bottom is uneven, perhaps strewn with large boulders, there will be zones where there is essentially no current. What this means for the nympher is that as the flies sink they are slowing down. The floating fly line and strike indicator in the surface currents are racing ahead of the nymphs and leader, and will soon pull the leader tight, *dragging the nymphs unnaturally fast through the water.* To counteract this, the fly line and upper portion of the leader must be repositioned to prevent this drag.

Drifting a Nymph with No Mend

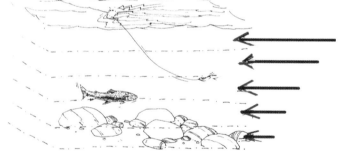

Water velocity decreases with depth

Because the current velocity near the stream bottom is usually much slower than at the surface, the sinking flies will be dragged unnaturally fast by the floating fly line and indicator.

A Critical Nymphing Skill: Mending the Fly Line

Ignore the following paragraphs at your own fly-fishing peril. If you want to be more than an average nymph angler, you absolutely must mend the fly line correctly, probably differently than you have ever mended before.

If there is one fly-fishing and nymphing skill which I see misunderstood and poorly executed it is mending the fly line. Actually mending the fly line AND the upper portion of the leader. I would rank ineffective mending as the Number One flaw for 80% of anglers who attempt to fish nymphs. Yes, even the experienced "experts".

Effective mending is pivotal to dead-drift nymphing success.
It all begins with a high rod tip position, at least head high.

I am passionate about effective mending, that is, the repositioning of the fly line and upper portion of the leader to prevent pulling the flies unnaturally fast through a fish's visual zone. It is often the difference between enticing a fish to strike or not. Mending can be the difference between a poor or mediocre fishing day and a spectacular day.

Prime Directive #2

Mend effectively. The mend is only effective when it removes the dragging tension in the leader so the flies drift as naturally as possible. For nymphs to sink quickly and drift drag-free, slack must be introduced into the leader. This is accomplished when the fly line and upper portion of the leader are repositioned *at the right time and upstream* of the nymphs.

I see three common errors in attempting the mend: 1) The mend is attempted too early after the cast is made. 2) The rod tip position is often too low, typically horizontal, at waist-high. 3) Too much of the fly line ends up repositioned off *to the side* of the strike indicator and drifting flies, allowing the fly line to race ahead of the flies, pulling them unnaturally fast, creating "drag".

Again, a mend is a repositioning of the *slack* floating fly line and upper portion of the leader. Because the cast is angled upstream, slack is created on the water's surface when the fly line starts to drift downstream in the current, back in the general direction of the angler. Though the fly line is slack *horizontally* in the surface, there is *vertical* tension on the leader as the fly line races ahead of the flies, pulling them and the leader to which they are attached too quickly downstream. Before tension can be most efficiently removed for the leader so the flies are not dragged, it is best to wait a few seconds after the cast before mending. Waiting allows for horizontal slack to form in the fly line. Then, the slack fly line and the upper portion of the leader in the fast near-surface part of the water column are repositioned almost directly upstream of the drifting nymphs.

When the mend is attempted immediately after the 45- – 60-degree upstream cast is made, the line is arrow straight. The only way a mend can be accomplished is to lift the rod tip to pull the line and leader toward the caster to create the horizontal slack necessary to reposition the

With the floating fly line to the side of the drifting indicator and leader — instead of behind them in the same current line — it will inevitably adversely affect the drift of the nymphs, hastening their drift, or slowing it.

After the mend is properly made, several feet, or more, of the fly line are positioned directly upstream of the indicator. Push the mend.

slack upstream of the flies. If the flies are cast to a specific current lane, directly on line with where a fish is suspected of being, the flies are pulled immediately out of this direct line when the rod tip is raised to create the slack fly line necessary for the mend. To prevent this, count slowly to three or four after the line hits the water after the cast before you mend the line.

The rod tip should be head-high as the mend is performed, not from the waist-high position. This lifts much of the slack line off the water, and very little effort is required to effectively reposition the line and upper part of the leader. I want the indicator to hop upstream a few inches to confirm that the mend has the potential to be effective all the way down to the indicator, delaying drag on the flies. It is important to completely mend the line and upper leader on the first attempt. The flies will not drift convincingly until the mend is fully completed. Repeated mending attempts during the drift postpone or kill the natural drift of the flies.

Effective Fly Line Positioning During the Drift

Another very common mending error is the repositioning of the fly line *to the side* of the flies instead of directly upstream of the flies, where the line should be. When the fly line is repositioned on the mend there are two directional components to the movement of the line: upstream AND away from the angler. So the fly line and upper part of the leader are pushed upstream and away in order for the line to be directly upstream of the nymphs, in the same current line. This allows for the best chance of an effective drag-free drift of the flies. Very few experienced anglers with whom I have fished understand the necessity of getting the line *directly* upstream of the drifting nymphs. Having the mended line off to the side of the fly may work when mending dry flies, but not for sunken nymphs.

One More Little Mending Detail

Several times I have mentioned that the upper portion — the first two or three feet of the leader — should be repositioned along with the floating fly line during the mend. Being not too far from the surface, the upper part of the sunken leader is being carried downstream by much faster currents than the slow-moving flies near the river bottom. So, the upper leader needs to be mended. To confirm that this happens the strike indicator should "hop" upstream during the mend. For whatever reason, most anglers think they are over-mending if the indicator is moved. The indicator *needs* to move a little to maximize the effectiveness of the mend.

The Mechanics of Effective Mending

At some point in our lives most of us have turned a jump rope for someone. I did, and I jumped rope, too. Not traditionally thought to be a manly or rugged thing to do, it was a great way for a young guy interested in girls to meet them by sharing a fun activity. Too young to drive a car, and not smart enough to know that walking a puppy was a sure way to meet girls, I did know how to turn a mean jump rope.

Think "turn the jump rope".

For years I had some difficulty conveying to my students and clients the proper movement of the rod tip to create a good mend of the fly line. I would demonstrate and encourage and suggest this and that, but too often students and guests just could not quite get it. That is until I suggested that they "turn the jump rope." That image resonates.

As I coach a newbie to mend I have them envision one end of a jump rope tied to a doorknob while they hold the other end. I have them see someone ready to jump the rope as they turn it over the head of the jumper. When it's time to begin fishing you will hear me direct the angler: "Cast. One, two, three, four. Turn the jump rope."

Once they get the hang of turning/mending the fly line like turning the jump rope I have them, then, angle the turn of the jump rope *diagonally* upstream. With this diagonal turn of the jump rope the movement has the two necessary directional components of an effective mend: upstream and away from the caster.

For proficient casters with experience I suggest that they do a mending roll cast. After the cast is made and a pause of a three or four count allows slack to form, I suggest they make a little diagonal upstream roll cast.

This will accomplish the same necessary fly-line position as the diagonal jump rope turn to get an effective drift of the nymphs.

It is often necessary to make a second mend during a single drift of the flies. The same mending mechanics are in play. Once the fly line and flies are much more than 45 degrees diagonally downstream of the angler it is usually ineffective to mend again unless you pull coils of line from the fly reel and simultaneously shoot (extend) and mend this excess line.

Stack Mending

"Stacking" mends is a technique whereby the fly line is mended by a series of mini roll casts. Multiple staccato, tiny mends are substituted for a big mend. I'm sure some anglers employ mend stacking with success and are believers. I have used stack mending in order to discover its advantages for me. The difficulty for me is that every time I execute a mend I'm temporarily out of control; there is a brief time during which if the strike comes I am moving counter to what I need to set the hook. Over a long career, I have had many occasions where the strike comes while I mend. By the time I react to change the direction of my rod tip to tighten the line it's too late. When trout are on the bite, and the fishing is fast and dependable, missing a few strikes is no big deal. However, steelhead fishing is a much different matter. In a full day's fishing there may be only one or two opportunities. If the strikes are missed because I was caught in the act of mending, there's a chance of going fishless. I seek to minimize mends, which entails making large mends that last through much or all of a complete drift of the nymphs. Of course, I sell my trout and steelhead clients on my rationale. Toward this end, I encourage my steelhead clients, in particular, to use switch or two-hand rods. Four- and 5-weight two-hand trout rods are now available in lengths to 12 feet. Long rods make big mends easier, and they can sweep a lot of slack line to tighten up quickly against a striking fish.

Tracking the Drift of the Flies

The cast has been made and the mend correctly executed. Now what?

The rod tip should track the drift of the strike indicator, a visual target easy to focus upon. More precisely, I want my rod tip to slightly precede the indicator. As the line and indicator passes downstream of my position I start to drop my rod tip to prevent the whole system pulling tight, which will stop my flies from drifting naturally along the bottom. I do this until I cannot drop the tip any farther. At this point the line will come tight, with the

flies ascending and swinging across the current. There is always a chance that an aggressive fish will smack the fly on the ascension or swing, especially is there are insects swimming or drifting to the surface to hatch. In fact, if I am consistently taking my nymphs on the swing, I will change the angle of the casts so they are 30 to 40 degrees to the current instead of 45 – 60 degrees. Mends are still necessary to sink the flies so they can eventually "rise" off the bottom just as the naturals do.

One other small detail when the fish are taking the swinging, tight-line nymph: no fingers on the fly line. The chance of a break-off on a big fish is a certain risk when the fly line is pinned against the cork, especially when small tippets and tiny nymphs are required. I set the drag precisely so that there is some "give" when the strike comes in order to cushion the impact, but there is enough resistance at the same time to bury the hook point.

An effective hook-set is facilitated by a slight "cheating", or leaning, in the downstream direction with the rod tip, in anticipation of the strike.

A Huge Challenge: the Proper Hook-Set

In my personal experience, I have not encountered 1 in 100s of experienced fly-anglers who set the hook correctly while fishing dead-drift nymphs. When the strike comes, most of the time they will not hook the fish!

The majority of fly-fishers began angling in our youths with bait and lures. When a bite or strike was detected we lifted the rod tip up and back to set the hook. In our early fly-fishing adventures, most of us started with dry flies and wet flies. When we detected a strike we lifted the rod tip *up and back* to set the hook. When this movement is repeated thousands of times over numerous years, this hook-setting movement becomes a natural ingrained reaction. A programmed habit.

As I begin my discourse about hook-setting with my clients and students, I always pose the same question: In which direction are the fish facing relative to the current? Just about everyone knows they face upstream into the current. It makes good sense. This is the direction in which food is drifting to them and it makes "breathing" easier as water flows into the mouth, past the gills, and exits behind the operculum.

The second question is always the same: If you choose to not harm the fish by hooking it when it grabs your nymph, in which direction should you move the rod tip in order to pull the fly away from the fish before it gets hooked, or pull the nymph out of the fish's mouth? Answer: Up and back.

Eric Gorman demonstrates good form as he sweeps the rod tip downstream and across, a high diagonal stroke, to set the hook.

My single greatest de-programming challenge is breaking experienced fly-anglers fishing nymphs of the up-and-back hook-set. They understand exactly what I am telling them about the error of their ways. However, even after I explain exactly in what direction to set the hook on the very next strike, the vast majority just can't do it. When the strike comes at an unpredictable time, their hook-setting programming causes them to do what they have always done. Their natural reflex out-paces their thinking process. Intellectually they understand. Reflexively they cannot help themselves.

This is often why beginners without ingrained bad habits will usually out-fish their expert companion when nymph fishing. The expert can get more strikes, but the newbie will land more fish.

Remember This and Catch More Fish

To successfully secure the hook into the fish's jaw or corner of its mouth the fly line and leader need to be pulled *downstream and across*. Actually, the best direction in which to move the rod tip is downstream on a high diagonal. If the rod tip is kept horizontal during the hook-set, there is a lot of fly-line drag as it is pulled through the water. This slows the rod tip during the stroke, so the line leader system does not tighten as quickly to firmly lodge the hook. Downstream on a high diagonal is the move.

Finally! Putting It All Together

Locate an expanse of likely fish-holding water: Walking-speed current, 3 – 7 feet deep, with some interesting bottom structure. If possible, start at the downstream end of the water to be fished, and plan to cover it methodically and thoroughly.

Casts are typically angled diagonally upstream. Shorter casts need not be mended since a high lift of the rod tip will lift all the fly line off the water. This is commonly referred to as "high sticking". If a little mend is wanted a small lift of the strike indicator to reposition a foot or two upstream is all that is needed.

When casts of 20 feet or more are made, a precision mend of the fly line and upper portion of the leader is needed to get a natural dead-drift of the nymphs. The mending stroke should be both upstream and away from the angler. As a result the fly line will be almost directly upstream of the nymphs. The indicator should be "hopped" upstream a bit to confirm that the mend has also repositioned the upper two or three feet of the leader.

The rod tip starts high after the mend happens. It tracks the strike indicator. To predispose the hook-set to be made diagonally downstream, I suggest nymphers actually lead the indicator *a little* with the rod tip. If the rod tip leads by too much it will pull the line and create drag.

If at any time the indicator does anything out of the ordinary — no matter how subtle — set the hook. It is a mistake to hesitate, thinking that a strike will be obvious. Many times it is not. I always remind my clients that there are no penalty points for setting the hook. Set it correctly and set it often.

Looks Tasty

It was salmonfly time on the Lower Deschutes. When these large stoneflies hatch mid-May into early June, incredible, memorable dry-fly fishing can be had.

When the fishing pressure is heavy or the trout get moody, the fish can opt to eat the migrating nymphs

In addition to repositioning the fly line upstream, the line is also pushed toward the bank on an effective mend. Think of the mend as a weak roll cast.

instead of the adult insects. This was the case the afternoon of this story. Having caught only a few good fish on dry flies earlier in the day, I changed to nymph fishing mid-afternoon. Casting through a reliable riffle the biggest fish of the day showed itself. It rolled up . . . and ate my fluffy yarn indicator. Bright green and fluorescent red with a golf ball silhouette, the indicator looked nothing like a salmonfly. Instinctively, I set the hook. To no avail, of course. I quickly switched back to a dry fly and made dozens of casts over the fish's position. To no avail, of course.

My good friend Jason Mariner prefers to use small balloons as strike indicators. They come in all the fun party colors, but he opts not to fish pink, red, or orange balloons because fish, both trout and steelhead, will occasionally try to eat these. He loses on two fronts. First, the fish typically cannot be coaxed on subsequent casts to take a nymph, having been startled or put off by the experience. Secondly, the balloon is popped, and time devoted to replacing it. Yellow, blue, and green seem to be the safe colors.

Drifting a Nymph with a Mend

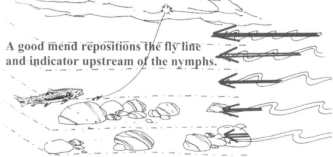

A good mend repositions the fly line and indicator upstream of the nymphs.

A proper mend repositions the fly line and indicator upstream of the flies to prevent dragging the nymphs. Multiple mends may be necessary during one complete drift of the flies.

Edible Strike Indicators

I was frustrated with my lack of nymph-fishing success in the early days of my fly-fishing career. However, I remained firm in my resolve to solve this puzzle. It only made sense that trout and char in rivers would have the

A large dry-fly indicator may be just what the fish prefer to eat.

easy and frequent meals provided by the insects and crustaceans that lived among the stones and rubble of the stream bottom. It was great fun to watch a fine fish surface to intercept my dry fly, and enjoyable, too, to feel the hard tug of a trout on my tight-line wet fly, but I knew with certainty that cracking the code on nymph fishing would increase my fish-catching success exponentially.

After a mediocre morning of fishing the Middle Deschutes River in central Oregon, I waded toward the river bank with my weighted stonefly nymph dragging in the shallows behind me. As I turned back and began to slowly reel in the fly I noticed a rainbow trout pecking at it, trying to pick it up, but unable to get a firm grasp on the nymph. If I had not been watching this I never would have known the fish was interested; I *felt* nothing in the line that conveyed the fish's interest. I wondered the obvious: How many trout had struck my drifting stonefly nymph today, and days past, and I never had a clue?

I had read stories of anglers who fished two flies, one a nymph and the other a bushy, buoyant dry fly on a dropper above it. It suddenly made more sense to me, the importance of *seeing*, not feeling, an indication of the quick interception and quick release of the artificial nymph. So, I tied a high-floating size-6 adult stonefly pattern on a short dropper line about three feet above my stonefly nymph. I massaged silicone fly floatant into the dry fly to waterproof it as best I could, and began casting into a nearby riffle. It was magic.

The same water that had given up no fish to my earlier nymphing efforts now held trout which I was able to catch because I could detect the strike. What a joyous epiphany. I landed more than a dozen trout that afternoon, and missed many others. And, there was an added bonus. Every now and then a rainbow came up to eat

my indicator! Even though there were no large insects on the water, or in evidence anywhere that day, certain fish wanted that dry fly. Though I had caught many more fish in a day, and I had certainly caught many bigger fish prior, this was the most satisfying fly-fishing I had ever experienced. That day marked the beginning of my lifelong focus on nymph fishing. It served as the cornerstone from which my nymphing knowledge and skills were built.

Four Techniques in One Cast

I wrote an article entitled "4 Fly-Fishing Techniques on One Cast" (*Flyfishing & Tying Journal*; Summer 2014). It all starts with a bushy dry fly and a small nymph suspended 30" – 36" below it. Some readers will have used or heard reference to the Hopper – Dropper set-up. Same thing, same idea. Commonly, I choose to fish a Bead Head Prince Nymph under a size-6 Stimulator or a Frankenfly Chernobyl Ant with a massive elk-hair wing.

As for the technique, the cast of the flies is angled upstream at 45 degrees, or even a little more straight upstream than 45 degrees. After waiting a count of three, I mend the line to prevent the system from prematurely dragging. Two techniques are being employed here: dead-drift dry fly and dead-drift nymphing. The dry fly is both enticing floating morsel and strike indicator. If the dry fly disappears, or zags, it is usually a sign the nymph has been eaten.

Once the drift of the flies is about 45 degrees downstream from my position, I mend the line again. The flies are beginning to drag. I mend to slow down the pace of the drag and straighten the line. Immediately I raise the rod tip to keep the waking dry fly from sinking. The wake can serve to call the fishes' attention to the flies. Meanwhile, the nymph ascends to the surface when the line tightens, and swings across the current with the dry fly. Depending on the current velocity, the nymph may be from 1 1/2 feet to just a few inches under the surface.

As for the additional pair of techniques, I am now fishing a skating/waking dry fly and a swimming/swinging nymph. For additional enticement I pulse the rod tip a few inches up and down *slowly*. At this point in the drift of the flies there is an excellent chance of watching fish track and strike the flies. A fish that follows or merely pecks at a fly can often be induced to strike it hard if the flies are gently twitched, as if they were alive. When caddisflies are hatching, and the pupae are swimming to the surface, and the adults are fluttering trying to lift off the water, this skating and swinging with a pulsing rod tip can create some very fast fishing.

High Sticking

When good holding water is within twenty feet, and the spot is deep and/or the surface choppy or rolling, I may need no more than a rod length of fly line beyond the rod tip. In fact, during the drift I may lift all of the fly line off the water with only the leader drifting in the current. This way my floating fly line cannot race ahead of the leader in the current to pull it unnaturally fast. My small-diameter leader is not pushed too quickly in the current, which would pull the flies down the river, perhaps alarming wary fish.

A longer rod translates into a higher, more distant reach of a controlled drift of the flies when "high-sticking", especially important in deeper water that cannot be very closely approached by wading.

After the cast is made — depending on the distance needed — I may find it necessary to mend the fly line in order to sink the nymphs quickly. As the system drifts toward me I can strip in some slack, while at the same time fully extending and elevating my rod arm. Depending on the dimensions of the piece of water I'm fishing, I may release and mend the slack line I have gathered as the line and flies had drifted toward me.

High sticking is particularly useful when fishing a zone surrounded by a variety of current speeds. For instance, a swath of water into which I am casting my nymphs in a rapids may be bordered by very fast currents which would race the floating fly line ahead of the nymphs and leader, pulling them. If I can get close enough to high stick this area, I can lift my fly line — at least most of it — off the water so it does not influence the drift.

No Mend Required

Because of the situation of the water I want to fish, or the stream bank's terrain, sometimes the presentation of nymphs must be made directly upstream of my position. One example of a common situation where I must cast directly upstream is when walking (or crawling) a cut bank.

If I do nothing but a straight-line cast, letting the line fully straighten in the air before the nymphs hit the water, the flies will eventually sink to the bottom into the fish's feeding zone. The fly line and leader are all in the same current line, so a mend isn't necessary. However, to enable the flies to sink quicker I will do a parachute cast. This is accomplished by casting high, then pulling back slightly once the line and leader have straightened in the air. When I pull the system back slack is created, so there is no tension on the flies as they plunk down. Thus, they descend quickly, and are near the bottom and fishing sooner.

Czech Nymphing

Czech nymphing, sometimes referred to as Polish nymphing, is a nymphing technique which is essentially high sticking with only a couple of feet of fly line, but often no fly line, beyond the rod tip. Some "Czeching" experts use a "leader" of 40 feet or more, most of which is spooled onto the reel whereby the fly line does not come into play during the presentation and drift of the flies. The flies are cast upstream, to drift through fishing zones very close to the angler's position. Rather than a dead-drift of the flies, they are pulled downstream slightly faster than the current. With the line being tight during the drift, the angler has an enhanced chance to feel the strike. A variety of strike indicators may be used though the leader is fairly tight during the drift. A popular type is the "sighter" strike indicator made by joining two sections of hi-vis fly-line backing, joined together by a loop-to-loop connection. At least some portion of the strike indicator is held above the water's surface during the drift. Using two different backing colors makes it likely at least one of the colors will be visible in varying light conditions.

Two or three flies are tied to the leader, at least one of which is heavy enough to sink the others very quickly.

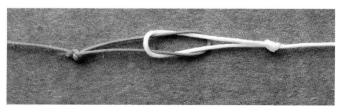

"Slighter" fluorescent backing indicator.

The French-style of Czech nymphing uses very light or unweighted flies, and the fishing water of interest is primarily 6 to 24 inches deep. The French-style presentation has the cast being directly, or near directly, upstream.

Spanish-style Czech nymphing can employ much longer casts to reach more distant fish-holding water.

Tenkara Nymphing

Tenkara is a Japanese method of fly-fishing. Only a rod, line, leader and fly are used. No fly reel.

A Tenkara rod carries no reel. The fly line — a fixed length — is secured at the rod tip. With longer sections of fly line the fish is landed by sliding it into the shallows or onto the bank, or by pulling in the line hand over hand.

There is growing interest in using Tenkara fly rods, which range from 8' 10" to over 14 1/2 feet. These telescoping rods can be compressed down into a compact 20-inch length, making for obvious travel advantage. Some models can be telescoped and locked to three different lengths. Typically, a short section of taperless fly line is attached at the rod tip. Fly-line sections commonly range from 8 – 20 feet. Hand-woven tapered lines of 10 1/2 and 13 feet are also available for better casting in a breeze. A couple of simple clips can be used to secure the fly line and leader to the rod. One is located on the butt and the other 18 – 24 inches above the rod grip, on the blank.

An inherent challenge for the Tenkara angler is that no line is retrieved during the battle with a fish. When it comes time to bring the fish to hand, or slide it into the net, the angler may have to reach very high to do

so if a longer section of fly line and a long leader are employed. Imagine casting just 20 feet of fly line and leader, and trying to land a fish with a 10-foot rod, or even a 13-foot rod. The best hope would be to slide the fish onto a beach or gentle-sloping bank.

Another possibility for gathering the line once the fish is hooked, and getting tired, is to grab the line with the off hand, then pull the fish in by hand. This is fine with small fish, but dangerous for a bigger trout that may have a bit of unused sprinting energy left. Every fly-angler has experienced lost fish when grasping the leader too soon in the fight, mistakenly thinking the fish was exhausted.

To get a feel for Tenkara fishing, clinch knot a section of old floating fly line to the tip of your standard fly rod.

Another consideration is playing a big trout on a *fixed* line length. Big fish can run a long way at high speed once hooked. With a fly reel I have had 15-inch rainbows tear off a hundred feet of line on their initial run in fast water. If I have no line to give during this sprint, it's a break off! Steelhead fishing is out of the question for all except the daring and lucky. Very lucky.

For the average angler Tenkara seems best suited to very short casts for small to medium size fish. For those considering getting a feel for Tenkara angling, do as I have done: to your standby trout fly rod clinch-knot a 6-foot section of old fly line to the rod tip, add a 6-foot leader, a small indicator, and a size 12 Bead Head Prince, or nymph of your choice. Find an approachable piece of fish-holding water 3 – 4 feet deep that can be covered with short casts, and give it a try.

The Other 10%

When fishing for trout and steelhead in rivers I employ the dead-drift technique 90% of the time. The other 10% of my nymphing time involves swinging or swimming the nymph on a tight line. Here, the strike will be felt, just as with a standard wet-fly presentation.

Jason Mariner demonstrates good fighting form during the battle with a fine steelhead: rod tip elevated, rod bent hard, and no hands or fingers on the reel or line.

In addition to using the tight-line nymph for trout, I use it in certain situations for steelhead. Having guided fly-fishers for steelhead for more than 30 years, I have discovered certain locations where steelhead are prone to taking a swinging nymph. At these chosen spots I try to prepare my clients to be ready for this possibility. If I don't mentally prepare them there is a high chance they will overreact to the strike, either pulling the fly out of the fish's mouth or breaking the tippet. In these select locations, then, we are fishing two nymphing techniques on one cast: dead-drift method on the upper and middle portion of the drift, and, then, the swimming/tight-line swing on the final portion of the drift.

When you think about the typical cast and drift of the flies while nymphing, we are virtually always fishing these two techniques. It's a mistake, I think, to pick up the nymphs too soon in order to recast. Let them linger on the chance a fish has followed the flies and may strike one if given the chance, or that the nymph has swung into a fish's visual zone directly below the angler. My guests hook a surprising number of both trout and

steelhead by letting their nymphs hang in the current. They are either distracted by the scenery, or awaiting the completion of their partner's fishing machinations, prompting them to pause, not to re-cast. Then, WHAM! Fish on!

Be patient through the entirety of the natural swing of the nymphs until they are directly downstream of you. Prepare to be pleasantly surprised occasionally. Maybe often.

Go Figure

We were anchored a short cast from the shore for lunch on a sunny October afternoon on the Rogue River. My two clients were seated and dining when we watched another drift boat drifting in our direction. While my guys were occupied I picked up one of the fly rods and began casting out into the river to signal to the oncoming anglers that we were intending to fish the water in front of us, and hopefully, they would give us wide berth. Courteously, the other boat stayed on the far side of the river. Before they drew even with our position one of the

Nearing the end of the long fight against a worthy rainbow,
Tom Clements finds his indicator at his rod tip. Time for the net!

My clients and I catch a significant number of steelhead
fall and winter as an egg fly swings after the completion
of the dead-drift part of the presentation. The challenge is
not to overreact on the hook-set.

fishermen hooked a steelhead. As we watched the show I let the two flies I was casting hang straight downstream, paying no attention to them. The water was fast enough that the two flies could not have been more than a few inches below the surface. Having very little line stripped from the fly reel, the stonefly nymph and my Bead Head Egg fly on the point were no more than 20 feet from the boat in water no more than three feet deep. A hanging, fluttering egg is anything but a natural presentation of a salmon egg as it slowly and naturally drifts along the river bottom. Fortunately I did not overreact when a steelhead grabbed the egg. Crazy. Fifteen seconds into the fight I handed the bouncing rod to Chuck Wagner who eventually landed a 7-pound psycho steelhead which defied common sense and ate a tight-line swimming egg. Go figure.

Nymphing Leaders for Stillwaters

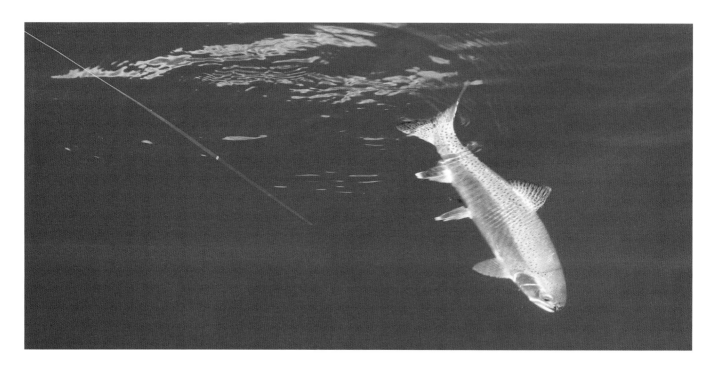

Effective stillwater nymph fishing is very gear intensive. Typically, I have four fly rods locked and loaded onboard my boat choice of the day; sometimes five. When fully armed, I have four different nymphing leaders in the mix. For those who choose not to be a One Trick Pony, but, instead, a fly-fishing "killing machine", leader design is an essential art.

Whereas much of nymphing in rivers and streams involves basically one leader set-up, the stillwater environments have much broader ranges of depths and fly presentations to be considered. Also in play are floating fly lines *and* an assortment of sinking lines. These drive leader designs.

We will arbitrarily designate depths of 15 feet or less as "shallow" water, and depths over 15 feet as "deep" water. From this point on, when I reference shallow water or deep water, 15 feet is the pivotal depth reference point. It is at this depth I may change my fly-line choice and my leader, too.

Nymphing Options in Stillwaters

Stillwater nymphing options include trolling, casting and retrieving flies, a combination of trolling and stripping, suspending nymphs, stationary, under an indicator, or a combination of stationary suspension with a periodic slow-strip repositioning of the nymphs. Choose your leader set-up depending on the particular method you choose and the water depth. Though not necessary in murky waters, in all situations I use *fluorocarbon* tippets.

It is crucial to know the water depth. Every consistently successful stillwater angler knows the depth of the water being fished. An electronic fish locator/depth finder is the easiest and fastest tool for this. Such equipment can be strapped in place, even on a float tube, using a nylon strap with a buckle, and some PVC pipe fittings.

The Basic Tapered Stillwater Leader

In shallow water situations when trolling with any type of fly lines, or casting nymphs with a full-sinking or sink-tip line, a 9-foot extruded tapered leader works just fine. When using a standard store-bought tapered leader for fishing ponds and lakes, I choose one with a small-diameter butt section, 0.022" or 0.021", to aid in the quicker sinking of my stillwater nymphs. And, I want the leader to be supple, not stiff. Flies need to exhibit realistic lifelike movement, not being pulled through the water on a rigid piece of cable. To assist in the freedom of movement

|— 30' —|

Stillwater tapered leader 9' - 12'.

Fly Line   8' - 13' Butt Section   12' Tapered Leader

0.025" diameter

20' - 25' Stillwater leader for fishing "Naked".

as the nymphs swim or hang in the water, I may reduce the tippet diameter that is normally recommended for the fly size. This can be particularly important when the sun is high, there is no breeze, and the water is very clear. Wary fish can be ultra picky, so a thinner-diameter tippet

When landing a fine fish when in my pontoon boat I have to improvise on how to position the fish for the photo.

enhances subtle "liveliness" and is harder to see. Additionally, I may add 3 or 4 feet of tippet to lengthen my leader to an overall length of 15 – 18 feet, adding more tippet with a Double Surgeon knot. If all these conditions — high sun, extreme clarity, and no breeze — are in play when I begin my fishing day, I may very well start with a standard 12-foot tapered leader instead of the 9-foot model, and lengthen it more if necessary.

The "Fishing Naked" Floating Fly Line Leader

A floating fly line is much easier to pick up off the water and re-cast, compared to a sinking fly line. Casting is definitely more pleasurable with a floater. Also, brightly colored floating fly line is an excellent strike indicator for detecting soft interceptions of flies. So, any opportunity for me to fish my floating fly line, I will choose it over my sinking lines.

Leader length for retrieving/stripping nymphs with a floating fly line is determined by the water depth. There is a simple mathematical formula I use to figure how long the leader should be.

It was in British Columbia I first heard the term "fishing naked" . . . at least outside of its literal image when alcohol and a dare might be involved. In BC "fishing naked" refers to fishing Chironomid pupae without employing a strike indicator. The Chironomid is tied to a long leader, cast out, then very, very slowly retrieved. This technique is a nice alternative to casting 20 feet of leader and tippet under an indicator.

The Canadian naked leader formula is: appropriate naked leader length = 1.25 X water depth. As an example, for fishing water 20 feet deep, leader length = 1.25 X 20' = 25'.

Successfully casting a 25- or 30-foot leader can be a challenge. An effective design is crucial to creating a leader that will fully extend with reasonable casting mechanics. After some trial and error, I have a design that works well for me.

For water depths exceeding 10 feet, tie a 0.025" butt section to the fly-line tip, and to this join a 12-foot standard tapered leader. The length of the 0.025" butt section is determined by taking the needed overall leader length and subtracting 12 feet (the length of the 12-foot tapered leader) from it. As an example, in 12 feet of water, the appropriate naked leader length = 12' X 1.25 = 15' overall length.

When casting leaders of 20 feet or more for "fishing naked", proper construction is imperative to combine good turnover and an effective presentation of the nymphs.

3' of 0.025" butt section + 12' tapered leader = 15' overall leader length

I realize that the water depths I am fishing throughout the day are variable. And inertia may prevent me from always diligently tending the details of my leader length. However, there are a couple of quick fixes to accommodate my malady. It takes less than two minutes to splice in a length of butt section material. Somewhere toward the middle of the butt section of the leader I am using I will cut it to splice in added length using blood knots to rejoin the leader sections. Or, with a little planning foresight I will carry another rod with a longer or shorter leader tied on and ready to cast.

Indicator Leader for Shallow Water

Suspending Chironomid pupae, Chironomid larvae, and nymphs like the Prince, Skinny Minnie, Horizontal Damselfly and Horizontal Dragonfly under an indicator, casted with a floating fly line, can be devastatingly effective. I want a leader design that allows my flies to sink quickly and cast reasonably well. While I need a bit of taper for extending the leader on the cast, my overriding concern is the rapid sinking of the flies. The other factor at play here is the ease or difficulty of repositioning the indicator as I slide it up or down the leader. This allows me to accommodate a variety of depths.

Indicator Leader Set-Up

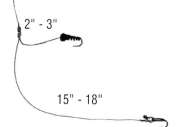

Indicator is set so point fly is suspended about 1' above the lake bottom.

2" - 3"

15" - 18"

I want a tapered leader with a small-diameter butt section, say 0.015" to 0.018". If I start with a 12-foot tapered leader out of the package, I will cut off the thick upper 3 feet before tying it to the floating fly line. In 15 feet of water, or less, I choose to lengthen or shorten my tippet in order to suspend the point fly about a foot off the lake bottom. A 6-foot tippet does not always fully extend very nicely, especially with two flies, but most of my casts do not exceed thirty-five feet for this technique, so this leader design is manageable.

Indicator Leader for Deep Water

I remember the first time I saw long-leader indicator Chironomid fishing on Roche Lake, BC. Those in the know were parked over 20 feet of water, and catching good numbers of fish. Without invading anyone's personal fishing space, I got close enough to easily hear the banter and conversation among the anglers who knew each other. While talking to each other several mentioned the depth, the same depth I was recording in my position, 20 feet. They were suspending their flies about a foot off the bottom, and I intended to do the same.

I hastily added several sections of tippet to my 10-foot leader in order to get about 19 feet between the

Long Indicator Leader Set-Up

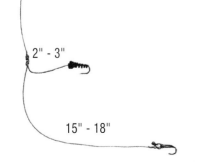

Slip-strike indicator slides down leader when fish is hooked.

2" - 3"

15" - 18"

indicator and Chironomid pupa. This seat-of-the-pants leader-construction project casted very poorly, complicated by the air-resistant strike indicator. The leader did not extend well, and after a clumsy cast was accomplished I wasn't always sure that the fly had not tangled with the leader on splash down or during the descent. I vowed to come up with a better design, which I did.

Starting with a 12-foot 3X leader, cut off the first 3feet of the butt section before tying the 9-foot remnant to the fly line. I cut off the thickest portion of the tapered leader for faster sinkability of the system. When fishing a Chironomid pupa or larva I most often fish a 4X or 5X tippet, appropriate for my most often used hook sizes, 12 – 16. If I am choosing to tie the fly to a 5X tippet, I will tie on sections of equal lengths 3X, 4X and 5X tippet material to arrive at the desired overall leader length, plus 2. The additional 2 feet of overall leader length allows me a little extra room if I should fish deeper water. See the following example.

For indicator fishing in deep water there is no substitute for the slip-strike type. These are a little tricky to set the proper amount of line tension, and they do wear out. Always carry extras.

When fishing 20 feet of water, like I did on Roche Lake, I want to suspend my fly at 19 feet, so I want an overall leader length of 21 feet (19' + 2' extra = 21')

21' leader length = 9' 3X tapered leader + 4' of 3X tippet + 4' of 4X tippet + 4' 0f 5X tippet

A slip strike indicator is the only type to use with a long leader. When set up properly the indicator will disengage on the strike or during the fight with the fish, and slide down the leader away from the rod tip. An indicator which is hard-fixed to the leader, incapable of sliding down once the fish is on the hook, will not work

Lesley Arle poses with a worthy stillwater rainbow before safely returning it to the lake.

with such a long leader. The indicator cannot be reeled through the rod's tip top.

Make Like a Scout

Leaders can be constructed in advance in the comfort of my home where my fingers are warm, the light is good, and I have time not dedicated to actually fishing. My hands are steady as I measure lengths and tie knots. If I have just broken off a large fish, or everyone around me is catching fish while I am trying to construct or modify my leader, my hands may not always be shake-free. So, prior to my next fishing trip, at home I can calmly put together a variety pack of leaders of different lengths and different terminal tippet diameters. I carefully coil them and place them in re-closeable sandwich bags. With an indelible felt tip I write the length and tippet diameter on each bag. My battle with inertia once I am on the water is not so great when I prepare my leaders in advance.

Locating the Fish in Lakes and Ponds

Locating prime spots to nymph fish trout and steelhead in rivers is usually a straightforward matter. Though fish can be found elsewhere in the river, when I "high grade" the easiest water for my clients and guests to catch fish I look for: depths of 3 – 7 feet, walking-speed current, and non-woody bottom structure. Assuming the fish are receptive to the nymphs being used, the combination of an upstream cast and a natural deep drift of the flies are deadly in these zones. On some of the rivers I fish, this specific water type represents only a fraction of 1% of the entire river area, so it is imperative to know, at any given water level, where these high-grade locations are found. For those who can "read the water" river fish can be pinpointed.

Without scuba gear, finding the fish at any given time in stillwaters can be a tricky endeavor, especially on big lakes. Lake and pond fish are nomadic. Some linger in an area for minutes or hours, and then move on in search of food, comfort, or protection. As conditions change, such as water temperature and sunlight intensity, the fish move. When an insect hatch ceases, the fish may cruise off in search of the next buffet. When the ospreys circle over the shallows, it's time to vacate. As the fish relocate, so must the angler.

Finding the Fish Starts at Home

As I begin to plan my next stillwater fishing trip I turn on my computer. The first thing I look for is a current fishing report. Knowing that virtually anyone who has a vested financial interest is "talking their own book", it is with the proverbial grain of salt that I consider what is reported. If I have a personal contact that has recent knowledge of the lake, I will call him. Even if he has not fished the water personally, he may have trusted friends who have. If the report piques my interest, in addition to the flies that may have charmed the fish, I want to know specifically where on the lake the action occurred. So, if I go to the lake and nothing obvious is happening, and I'm short on clues, I will migrate toward the location that produced for my friend, or his friends.

If I have to rely solely on the Internet for my fishing report I am sifting through the text to discover if the "where" is mentioned. Sometimes it's there. I am also interested in any photos. Not to see the fish, but to see the surroundings and landmarks that may be a tip off.

Next stop: YouTube. Many anglers want to wow the viewers with their fishing exploits, so they make a video. During the fishing activity I am, again, searching the surroundings, trying to glean any clues. Occasionally, the video angler or cameraman may indicate the location being fished.

Keep a Folder

It is impossible to remember all I will need to know to successfully fish a new lake. So, I record my pertinent Internet information on a yellow legal tablet. Very old school. These pages will be the first occupants of my file folder for the lake, or lakes, of my upcoming trip. More documents will soon follow.

Bathymetric maps are quite useful. They provide a very quick overview of a lake's depth profile. Features like submerged channels, shoals, and drop-offs can be located at a glance. Stream inlets may be located, too, where fish may gather at pre-spawn, or are drawn there because of more attractive water temperatures at certain times of year.

Also in the folder will be documents that pertain to food and fishing supplies, travel directions, passport or visa, and accommodations. Once the fishing has begun, I keep a diary of the day's fishing events and lessons. More about the specifics of journaling later.

Bathymetric Maps

An alternative to doing my own underwater topography reconnaissance with scuba gear is to obtain a bathymetric map of the lake I am going to fish. Such a map shows a depth profile. Assuming I have few clues about where to begin fishing my chosen stillwater, I study this map to

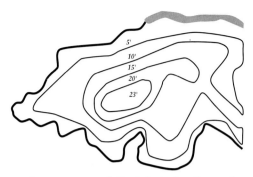

Bathymetric maps reveal the lake's depths and contours, offering clues about where fish may be found.

discover areas that range from 8 – 20 feet deep, what I consider the prime fishable zone. With this information I can choose a launch site closest to the area, or areas, on the lake I want to search.

Contour maps can reveal shoals, channels, drop-offs, and springs. These are all likely areas where fish may patrol or concentrate. Once a hot spot is located, the coordinates can be programmed into a GPS unit. These coordinates can be recalled in order to find the same lake bottom feature or hot spot in the future.

It may be possible to locate an online map of a lake where fairly accurate GPS coordinates can be found by moving the computer screen cursor over the map. I place the cursor over a river channel, spring, shoal, or other feature of interest. Then, the coordinates can be programmed into my GPS device. Once on the lake, the GPS unit will lead me to where I want to go. It's hard to know the accuracy of the map readings and the accuracy of my GPS, so I might need to fine-tune my position on the lake with the aid of an electronic depth finder. As I crisscross the zone of interest on the lake, noting the depth changes and bottom contours displayed on the screen of the depth finder, I have an excellent chance of

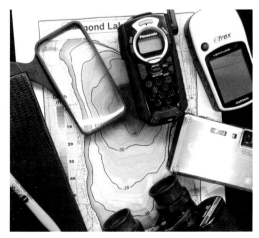

Important fishing tools: bathymetric map, GPS, two-way radio, binoculars, and waterproof camera.

pinpointing the bottom feature I'm searching for. Once I have discovered the exact location, the new coordinates can be entered into the GPS.

Vehicular Pursuit

While wading may well be a viable option for successfully fishing streams and rivers, it is a rarity on lakes. A floating craft is necessary. There are numerous choices. All floating manner of tubes, pontoons, and boats have their pros, and all have their cons. Let's consider them one at a time.

Float Tube

For those wanting to get into lake fly-fishing in a hurry with minimal cost, a "U"- or "V"-shaped inflatable float tube is the way to go. For savvy shoppers, the tube and the fins to propel it can be had for less than $100 American. Deflated, a float tube is easily stored, transported, or carried. It is a great craft for very precise, variable-speed trolling.

As for the float tube cons . . . It can take a very long time to travel a significant distance. If I must launch my tube a quarter mile, or more, from where I want to fish, it can be a long, tiring kick to get there. And that means a long, tiring kick to return to the launch site. Especially when working against the wind!

In a relatively inexpensive and quite portable inflatable craft Patrick Gorman can get to the fish with maximum nymphing options available, including precision trolling.

I had a situation on Montana's Clark Canyon reservoir where a powerful wind arose in two heartbeats. As I flexed my fins hard to get to the shore I had swells coming over the top of my float-tube backrest. Fortunately I was less than a hundred yards from the bank, as were my friends. The prudence of carrying or wearing a safety floatation device was more evident than it had

ever been. Bucking a strong wind on a lake is best done with young legs.

Inflatable Pontoon Boat

Available starting at a few hundred dollars, one-person inflatable pontoon boats are very popular.

Though the fishing is done with fin control, most are set up with oars to cover reasonably long distances in a short period of time. With the feet out of the water there is less water drag while the boat is rowed. Compared to fin propulsion to cover significant distance, not much effort is required to row. And, it is certainly easier to row against the wind than kick against the wind.

A versatile and popular craft, many inflatable pontoon boats are equipped with oars for quick travel time from Point A to Point B, which is a big plus when the wind is blowing.

On the downside, because a pontoon boat sits higher on the water than a float tube, it is more easily pushed by the wind. Trying to hold stationary in a given spot is a challenge. Some boat models come with an anchor frame, and this is helpful for holding steady.

I am not into seeking out and repairing leaks in an inflatable pontoon boat. I have participated in such repairs, and will not participate in the future. That's me. I am sure many who own these watercraft have never had to do a repair.

Once deflated, these boats are a bit cumbersome to store or transport. If the boat has an aluminum frame, this goes up by a power of 10 if your fishing vehicle is not a pick-up truck.

Hard-Shell Pontoon Boat

I am a get-there-and-throw-the-boat-in-the-water sort of guy. I want to dedicate no time to inflation or assembly, and absolutely no time to an undiscovered leak which must be repaired. God made the hard-shell pontoon boat with me in mind. I transport it strapped to the roof rack of my 4Runner. I can nest a second one on top of the first and drive easily at highway speeds. The boat is 75 inches long, and weighs less than 40 pounds. With a minimal drag design, I can row it faster than most inflatable pontoons. I have one set-up to accommodate an anchor. The manufacturer warns against it — just as I am warning you — but I use it on rivers often. And, this is a very durable boat.

The downside? Hmmm, can't pull a water skier.

My preference in a pontoon boat is a Hobie hard-shell model. 75 inches long, about 40 pounds, and never needs to be inflated or deflated: the ultimate lazy-man watercraft. Joann Severson is preparing to go in pursuit.

Car-Top Boat or Pram

Car-toppers and prams are very practical boats, and very popular. These are very stable platforms from which to anchor and cast. No waders required, and fatigue from getting from Point A to Point B is minimal, especially if a motor is used. On lakes where motors are not allowed, oars easily accomplish the job.

Smaller boats can be transported in an open pick-up bed. If not, a trailer is required. More expense and storage space are necessary when the boat is home. Many anglers find no problems with these requirements.

A significant part of my fish-searching and fish-catching game plan centers on trolling when I have minimal clues about where the fish are and the flies they will eat. One person in a boat propelled only by oars or a motor cannot effectively troll. Yes, you can troll and catch some fish, but you cannot troll *effectively* in order to maximize all the fish-catching opportunities available. Trolling is a very nuanced art, full of stops and starts, and slow manipulations of the fly. This cannot be accomplished in any boat not propelled by fins. And — no — no one is good enough to do this with a foot-controlled electric motor. Nice try, but *el nopo*.

Steve Fitzsimon will be sitting high and dry in his aluminum cartop boat. These are utilitarian, lightweight casting platforms.

Drift Boat or Dory

As a river guide often picking my way through whitewater dangers in Oregon, I have a drift boat. It has design similarities to dories used in rivers and coastal saltwater. Because I already have a drift boat for my river work, it is available for fishing stillwaters, too.

When I have guests fishing with me, it is less hassle and more productive if I can put them in the boat for transport to the fishing, with no exertion or preparation on their parts, no safety concerns, and I am with them to coach, net their fish, and take memorable photos. I can easily accommodate two anglers; three, if I must.

My drift boat can act as Mother Craft. If I have guests who want to fish from a float tube pontoon boat, I can load them into my drift boat with the craft and deliver them to a distant destination, depositing them on the shore. Then, I return and pick them up.

Designed to negotiate whitewater on western rivers, the drift boat doubles as a stillwater craft capable of carrying multiple anglers and lots of gear.

If I fish by myself, sometimes my drift boat is convenient to carry a lot of camera gear, lots of rods, and new flies to experiment with. I do not need to don waders, put on fins, and slowly get to where I want to be. My top priority is not to maximize my fish count, but to get some photos and try new flies for non-trolling methods.

Canoe

I once owned a 17-foot square-stern aluminum canoe. I could put a little motor on the back, and I added oarlocks so I could actually row it instead of paddle. It was necessary for me to have a second person in the boat to drop the bow anchor when I dropped the stern anchor. Wasn't a very stable craft for all the moving and fidgeting I found necessary. Standing up was always a challenge. Had to troll without holding onto the rod. Rarely used it. Sold it five years after purchase. Have never missed it. Not once.

This Canadian on Edith Lake made his canoe much more fishing-friendly by equipping it with oars. For some of us, fishing from a canoe with only paddles, especially in a breeze, is a once-in-a-lifetime experience. Never again!

Raft

If you like inflating and deflating and doing patching repairs, a little raft may be for you. They can be quite inexpensive, which is a plus for those on a budget. This is an easy craft to carry and launch.

A raft set up properly for fishing two or three people will have a solid floor and a rowing frame. This will not be an inexpensive craft like a one-man inflatable. Larger rafts, properly equipped, will require a trailer to carry it. This is a versatile boat which can also be used on rivers. As for running whitewater with big standing waves, drift boat passengers have a better chance of staying dry during the ride.

Power Boat

To get somewhere in hurry on a big lake, a power boat is the craft. Some spacious models will easily accommodate four fly-anglers.

These boats have the same limitations as prams. Car-toppers, dories, and drift boats. On some lakes gas-powered motors are not allowed.

Large engine-powered boats are comfortable for travel, and you can even have lawn chairs and a refrigerator onboard. However, they are not so convenient when moving frequently from spot to spot.

Searching for Fish Pre-Launch

There's a hackneyed phrase which says "You cannot catch fish where they aren't." I have a specific game plan once I arrive at the lake. I resume Job One — finding the fish. I have done my homework before the trip, but it now continues on Game Day as soon as the lake is in sight.

Before I throw my boat into the water I scan the lake, searching for clues to locate the fish. I am looking for rise activity, insects on the water or in the air, insectivorous birds patrolling a specific area, and other anglers, especially concentrations of anglers. As for geographical features, I make note of bays, points, islands, shoals, and creek mouths which will be likely points of interest to explore.

In order to jump right into fish hunting on the lake or pond I have all my fly rods strung and ready to cast. No fishing time wasted here. With four or five rods this can save a half hour of assembly time. Most of the time my boat of choice is a hard-shell pontoon boat. No inflation or leak repairs required. More fishing time saved.

Tally Ho, Here I Go

The next phase of Job One is set in motion with launching my boat. I have determined before hopping into my boat exactly where I want to go. If I see a concentration

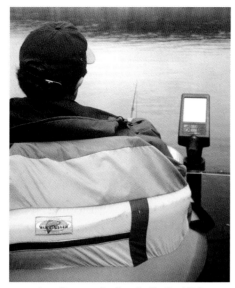

An electronic depth finder/fish locator acts as underwater eyes. An indispensable stillwater tool.

of anglers, I am heading in their direction. If I see rising fish, I am definitely cruising that way. A nearby shoal, bay, or tributary may beckon if these first two possibilities are not available.

Once on the water I employ two more fish-locating tools. First, I turn on my electronic fish locator/depth finder. I want to know the water depth when I have moved a short distance from the launch site. This tells me what sinking line to select to troll the nymphs as I head toward the initial destination on the lake. And, of course, I am not only checking depth with my electronics but also watching for indications of fish around me. Secondly, I strip line from the reel so that the flies trailing slowly behind me are searching for fish, too. At this point I am multi-tasking to the max — visually searching, electronically searching, and searching with flies.

One of the benefits of trolling as I search is that I do not need to watch my line to detect a strike. My eyes are free to survey what is going on the lake, and watch my electronics screen.

Underwater Eyes

An electronic depth finder/fish locator is an absolute "must" piece of equipment. I do not know of many consistently successful stillwater fly-anglers who do not rely on electronics when fishing large or new lakes. Knowing the exact depth of the water being fished can be absolutely critical for fly-line selection, leader length, and for precisely suspending a fly under an indicator. Noting depth changes and bottom contours is important in locating fish. There are times I need to fish over a particular

depth range because today the fish are choosing to station themselves in water that is 12 to 16 feet deep, for instance.

As for the fish-locating feature of this tool, it does not enable me to pinpoint a fish, cast to it, and catch it. Fish are usually on the move, so as soon as I get a fish's location on the screen it is elsewhere by the time I make my cast. What is useful is knowing there *are* fish in the area. Sometimes I will see a preferred depth at which many of the fish are suspended as they cruise, but most of the time fish are spread out vertically in the water column.

One more important detail my electronics give me is the water temperature. Locating cool water in the summer, or warmer water in the spring and fall, may guide me to the fish.

Important information on the screen: depth, contours, water temperature, and fish in the immediate vicinity.

Temporary Blindness

A few years ago, in the midst of a week-long fishing trip in British Columbia, I got a hot tip about Jimmy Lake. The typical story: big fish, and lots of them. The fishing equivalent of a treasure hunt. And, as with any good treasure seeking, it would prove to be a not-so-easy location to find for a Yankee on a maze of roads without good signage. All these contribute to the intrigue, of course.

Once I found the lake my anticipation was near overload. This would be the stuff of fly-fishing movies perhaps. Because there were only a couple of anglers on the lake I was not going to get many clues about where to fish. I would be relying mainly on my electronics. Because Jimmy was a lake that had been added on a whim during the trip, I had had no time to do adequate research on this water before I departed home. Fishing reports and a contour map are very useful aids, in addition to adequate driving directions.

When I finally arrived at the lake late afternoon there were a dozen campers. The fishing was apparently over because everyone was in camp. I would have the lake to myself, which is both good and not so good. I could go anywhere I chose without interfering with other anglers, but there would be no hints about where to fish. I would have no bloodhounds leading me to the fish.

As I began to make my way around the perimeter of the lake trolling a Midnight Bugger I could see only the occasional fish blip on my screen. In between glances at my electronics I was looking for rising fish, insects on or over the water, swallows working an area of hatching insects, or anglers who might decide to launch a boat to join me. I watched the depth recordings on the screen and noted drop-offs and bottom structure, attempting to stay in the zones where the depths were reasonable, not too shallow and not too deep.

Waiting in Ambush

When I visually survey a lake, both before and after I launch, I search for ambush points, areas where fish may concentrate or travel near, around, or through seeking food. If I have no reason to focus my fishing efforts on a specific area I will begin to explore these likely zones by fishing them. Scanning the "lay of the land" I look for small bays, stream inlets, points of rocks or land, rock slides, cliff faces, and shorelines of cattails and bulrushes. Fish will often patrol shorelines with reasonable depth in search of both terrestrial and adult aquatic insects which fall or are blown into the water. Also, windblown hatching aquatic insects may be swept to the shore where fish will

In the Catholic tradition, gluttony is one of the Seven Deadly Sins. This gluttonous largemouth bass grabbed a fly before it finished swallowing his bluegill meal.

find them concentrated, easy fare. As you might guess, shoreline fish can be quite susceptible to being caught on a dry fly.

Shoreline areas with adequate depth, let's say 8 – 15 feet, are good places to troll. Such areas usually allow sunlight to penetrate to the bottom to promote plant growth where insects and crustaceans can thrive. So, not only is there the possibility of food from the shoreline vegetation but also the nymphs, larvae and crustaceans inhabiting the shallow waters nearby.

In the shallows there may also be large mats of big-leaf water plants like water lilies, whose floating pads may form a massive mat. Because these plants can serve as havens for fish foods, and also offer a bit of hiding-out protection for the fish when danger draws near, trolling or casting to the edges of these water plants can definitely produce fish. For fish seeking shade from a high sun, such plants offer a cool canopy to rest or hide under. For those species like largemouth bass, crappie, and bluegill, mats of lily pads are a magnet, excellent ambush areas for both fish and the stillwater angler.

Shoals are another feature in a lake's topography where fish may be found. I think of a shoal as an underwater island, higher in elevation than the surrounding lake bottom. Productive shoals have a lot of plant growth on them. Fish will cruise along the edge or up onto the shoal to feed. On light-colored shoals fish can be seen cruising as they forage. A good strategy is to park away from, but within easy casting distance, to a shoal in order to cast onto it or along its edge, and retrieve the flies. It certainly adds to the interest of the game to watch fish swimming in your fishing zone. Trolling the shoal's edge can also be very productive.

Shoreline vegetation holds the possibility of underwater foods among the stems and roots, and also airborne goodies that might drop into the water on the next breeze.

Shoals are large expanses of shallow water surrounded by deep water. If the substrate is lightly colored, cruising stillwater fish may be sighted and targeted by the angler. Pass Lake, BC.

I love to fish little bays or coves. I anchor at the mouth of these and spray my casts in a 180-degree arc. These areas can also offer shelter from the wind when maneuvering, anchoring, and casting on the main lake can be tedious or impossible. On busy smaller lakes, with lots of boat and fishing commotion, fish may retreat to quiet coves and bays in search of a quiet zone to feed and feel safer. In addition to casting and retrieving flies, suspending nymphs under an indicator is another obvious method here from my stationary boat.

An island's perimeter is a good place to troll. I watch my depth readings to stay in the prime 8- – 15-foot zone. As I go I am looking for likely looking places to cast and retrieve a fly, or fish an indicator when I make a second pass around the island or return another time. I am always taking mental notes.

Inundated timber and submerged logs can create aquatic insect habitat and provide protective shelter for the fish. Again, warm-water species love cover. When in pursuit of these fish, areas of timber and logs are logical choices. A great example of a lake with an abundance of both flooded trees and submerged wood is Oregon's Crane Prairie. In the late 1920's a large timbered meadow was dammed at its downstream end to create a shallow 4,000+-acre reservoir with a shoreline perimeter exceeding 22 miles. The submerged wood provides excellent habitat for dragonfly nymphs, producing a world-class population of these insects, which in turn help

grow "cranebows" exceeding 10 pounds. In addition to brook trout and rainbows, years ago some law-breaking character illegally tossed largemouth bass into the lake. The bass numbers boomed in this woody wonderland.

Points of rocks or land protruding out into a lake can direct cruising fish into a narrow line of passage around the point. Casting and trolling near these features can be productive. And, the same is true where rockslides or old lava flow slopes into the depths. Davis Lake, at the southern terminus of Oregon's Century Drive, has a well-known boat launch site and fishing area referred to as The Lava Flow, situated along the lake's northeastern shoreline. Here the bottom drops off quickly into an area where the rainbows can always be found, patrolling the area for its abundant insect life. The depths just off the ancient lava flow are adequate to stay cool enough year-round that many trout will congregate here. Just south and adjacent to the lava slope is a large shallows with reeds and cattails. Just like Crane Prairie, a few miles to the north of it, Davis Lake had largemouth bass illegally introduced. They tend to take up residence among the vegetation jungle of this shallow region. So, it's possible to fish for rainbows in a prime area of the lake, then move a few hundred yards to pursue bass.

At certain times of year trout may gather at the mouth of a lake's inlet stream. In addition to the possibility that the stream may carry food into the lake, late winter and early spring find rainbow trout seeking moving water in which to spawn. Brown trout will do the same in the fall. If the lake warms to uncomfortable temperatures in the heat of summer, an inlet's flows may be comfortably cooler, and attractive to fish. At such times, a perceptive angler may seek out the creek or river mouth as an ambush station.

Lake outlets are locations where drifting food items may collect. The outlet acts as a funnel into which insects with poor mobility are swept, especially when they are in helpless hatching activities. For the attuned fish, the current created by the lake outflow acts as a conveyer belt delivering food to it as the fish holds its position, minimizing its energy expenditure while dining.

Listen and Learn, Little Grasshopper

Sound carries extremely well on a lake, and can actually be amplified *when the surface is calm*. It's all about physics. Because the air is cooler at the water's surface than it is a few feet above the surface, sound traveling across the lake is bent, or refracted, downward. Besides being bent downward the sound waves are also reflected off a *flat* surface, adding to the volume of the sound.

When the lake is calm I listen for rising, splashing fish, whirring fly reels with a fish pulling line , and conversations among fishermen. Potentially, information about fishing success, techniques, and flies may be heard.

Many successful stillwater anglers do not want to share the details of their success while on the lake. To do so can draw a crowd into his immediate geographical area. And, not everyone has respect for another angler's personal space. Thus, the understandable reluctance to share. But, if Mr. Success is fishing with a friend, when he talks with his companion about his fly or technique — even in hushed tones — there's a possibility the conversation may be heard at significant distance if the lake is dead calm. Listen and learn.

Roche Lake Cluster and Talk Fest

Kamloops, British Columbia is lake fishing Ground Zero zone. There are dozens of quality fly-fishing lakes within an hour of the city. It serves as an excellent fishing base camp, with all the necessary amenities close by.
Roche Lake is a very popular rainbow trout fishery within forty minutes of Kamloops. Spanning more than 300 acres, it's a good size lake able to accommodate a lot of anglers. A boat with a motor or oars is preferred to quickly move from place to place to discover where the fish are concentrated, and to move elsewhere on the lake as the fishing changes throughout the day.

In June 2010 Roche Lake was a puzzle with very few clues for me. The electronics indicated that there were many fish around me in certain locations, but they were nobody's fools. In addition to my own experimentations

Woody structure in lakes and ponds offer cruising fish the possibility of food, such as dragonfly nymphs, and some element of protection in an emergency.

Roche Lake, BC. Lots of fish, lots of fishermen. If boats are clustered in a small area, there's a good reason.

with flies and techniques, I had hoped to rely on other anglers providing me with some clues about how to entice the trout. They were little help. I saw very few bent rods throughout the entire fishing day, with the exception of a boat with a guide and his client who caught fish on a semi-regular basis. The guide was constantly monitoring his depth finder/fish locator as he changed the boat position from time to time. Though observing the guide and angler did not improve my success that day, it did give me hope that the fish could be caught on Roche *if* the puzzle pieces could be assembled correctly. I knew I would eventually return to successfully challenge the rainbows in this lake.

A year later I returned to Roche Lake with my friend Jeff Hilden. An experienced and resourceful angler, Jeff is a valuable scout and companion as we try to discover where the fish are and how to catch them. Our Day 1 strategy was to head for a concentration of anglers, wherever that might be, watch, and listen. This little plan can take some discipline for those of us that naturally lapse into wanting to fish and experiment along the way to our ultimate destination. The danger is arriving at the Red Zone — where the angler cluster may be located — too late. Fish can move or go off the bite if you dawdle. This is where discipline is needed for guys like me who want to ponder and experiment. So, it's put my oars in the water, not my fly. Stay on task and get to the end zone.

As an aside, the previous year I had not arrived at the lake early in the day. I had not launched my boat until noon. This can be a fatal error sometimes. So, Jeff and I were on the water by 8 a.m. Because I tend to stay up late into the night journaling about my fishing day and preparing my gear for tomorrow, I tend to get out of bed a little later the next morning than I should. Arriving at the lake at daybreak is rarely necessary, but noon is too often too late. You snooze, you can lose.

With anglers catching fish nearby on a regular basis it pays to watch, listen, and learn. Sound carries very well on lakes.

Toward the south end of the lake there were more than a dozen assorted fishing crafts, all patrolling or anchored in just a few acres of water. At any given time it seemed someone had a fish on. This was promising. And, to our delight, there was frequent conversation. In particular, there were four friends (whom we later met) who rendezvoused each year for a week or so at Roche Lake, their annual Boys Fishing Holiday. Each had his own car-top boat, and all were anchored within easy talking distance of each other. They frequently talked to each other about what fly was working, or not working. So, like Little Grasshopper, I listened and learned.

In addition to fly information, I was able to mentally map out their exact positions, relating them to a nearby little island. If I should returned there with my choice of locations to anchor, I could closely locate the footprint of each of these boats. Also, I slowly moved in and around the Red Zone, I could note the water depth, about 20 feet. Like the Four Friends, everyone I could see was fishing a Chironomid pupa suspended under an indicator. It was "heave it and leave it". And, other friends fishing throughout the cluster were sharing info with each other — and us inadvertently — throughout the morning, making our jobs of Where, How, and With What very easy. Jeff and I caught some very good fish as a result of watching and listening.

Subsequent fishing on Roche Lake the next day, and again in 2013, was very successful as a result of our reconnaissance.

When all the puzzle pieces are fitted together, good things happen.

The Red Zone: A Moving Target

Jeff and I returned to Roche Lake on Day 2. Though we arrived earlier than the previous day, the Gang of Four was already in their positions. Interestingly, each was anchored in a different location than the day before.

Today they had all moved what I estimated to be about eighty feet farther south and east. I could not argue with their choices, since someone among them always seemed to have a fish on. Their combined experience at Roche Lake, their continual exchange of information, and their fly-fishing skills made them excellent teachers to imitate. So, if they determined that yesterday's Red Zone was not optimal today, they searched for and discovered today's Red Zone. It can be a moving target. There are times that fish go off the bite, but there are also times where the fish are relocating to eat elsewhere.

As the fishing slowed down for everyone later in the morning, one of the Four Friends pulled anchor to search for a new Red Zone. He eventually found it, and started catching fish. His friends saw him at a distance with a bent rod on several occasions, so they too pulled anchor and joined him.

When the fishing action fades in an area I am fishing, I don't assume the fishing is finished for the day. I go in search of a new location where the fish are concentrated and in the mood. As I go I troll, looking and listening for information that will lead me to the next Red Zone.

Should I Stay or Should I Go Now (The Clash, 1982)

The decision to stay put in a proven fish-catching location, or to pull anchor and relocate is a crucial one. Sometimes changing flies or the fly-fishing technique — or both — while staying put is the best choice. Other times, it's best to go on the hunt for willing fish. A few years ago, late June, my angling friend and fraternity brother Chuck Wagner and I were fishing Diamond Lake, a highly productive Oregon stillwater. The fishing can be stellar, with the potential for some big catch numbers. In recent years the Oregon Department of Fish & Wildlife has planted more than 200,000 rainbow trout there annually. If the large trout were not subjected to a daily catch-and-kill massacre throughout the entire fishing season, Diamond could be one of the West's premiere public trophy trout lakes. Perhaps, THE best. Oh, well . . . .

Part of the logical game plan — again — was to seek out the concentration of fly-anglers to discover if they had located the concentration of dining trout. Fly-anglers on Diamond Lake will be the minority. Bait-fishing is the choice of the masses there. Just like birds of a feather tend to flock, human nature has it that fly-anglers tend to seek each other's company. At least they seek to be in the general proximity of other fly-fishers where they have a chance to watch and listen to others using the same angling methods.

Big trout draw big crowds at Diamond Lake.

It was not difficult to find other kindred fishing spirits at the lake's south end. These "hounds" had done some of our reconnaissance for us, picking up the scent and leading us to the fish. As we approached the pack we could see several bent rods. Yes! In Chuck's power boat we weaved in and around the boats, making sure we did not trespass on anyone's personal fishing space. While some fishermen were trolling flies, most were fishing a Chironomid under a strike indicator. Chironomids seemed a logical choice since adults were in the air and landing all over our boat.

In the first two spots we anchored to begin our fishing day, we got no strikes. Was our lack of success due to our specific locations? Was it our fly choices? Was it our tippet diameter or leader length? Were we too late? Having launched early afternoon because of travel circumstances, perhaps the bite was fading. As evidence for this we watched the number of anglers dwindling, as they piloted back to the take-out point.

For our third anchored location we found a position over patches of shallow weed beds. Casting around the vegetation we finally got some strikes, and landed a few fish. We experimented with fly patterns and techniques, but a little black Chironomid pupa with a silver bead, fished under an indicator, served us well.

Soon only a very few boats remained in our immediate area. One that did remain was a motor-propelled drift boat with a man and woman fishing from it. Their method of choice was casting and stripping the fly, not Chironomids under an indicator. And, they were hit-and-

run nomads. When I began watching them for the first time they anchored not far from us, and began to cast. In a few minutes they combined to hook at least three fish. They methodically cast to all positions around the clock, then pulled anchor again. I watched the captain watch the shallow lake bottom as he searched for a new anchoring position. I don't know exactly what he was looking for. Vegetation? Deeper water? A channel? A drop off? Cruising fish? I still don't know, but whatever it was he would find it, drop anchor, and they would start fishing again.

At their second observed location, the lady immediately hooked a fish; then he did. They knew something about tracking down the fish and enticing them to bite. Even after so many anglers had given up for the day, these nomads knew that there were fish still wanting to eat. These anglers knew that Red Zones were still out there to find, and now that so few boats remained in our immediate area they were free to roam as they would without having to worry about interfering with others fishing.

Over the course of the next hour I watched the man and woman repeat the anchor/cast/catch a few fish/move routine over and over. In the meantime Chuck and I would get the occasional strike and a fish, but nothing like their success.

During this time I landed a good rainbow on a Chironomid and used my stomach pump to steal its lunch before I returned it to the lake. When I squirted the stomach contents onto a yogurt lid I discovered dozens

Using a stomach pump to rob a trout of its most recent meal I found a single leech and scores of Chironomid pupae. This made fly selection easy.

of Chironomid pupae and a single leech that just about spanned the diameter of the lid. This indicated that our Chironomid pupae flies were an adequate match for the naturals, and the fish were feeding hard on these. So, why were the people in the drift boat so successful with casting and stripping flies to catch fish. Chironomid pupae can slowly wriggle a tiny bit, but they cannot swim, especially at the quick retrieve pace used by Mr. & Mrs. Nomad. Were they fishing a leech pattern?

I tied on a leech and began mirroring the retrieve timing and strip speed and length of the other anglers. I cast in a variety of directions. Nothing. Tried a second leech. Same routine. Nothing. Was it possible we had depleted our Red Zone of willing trout? Those in our immediate vicinity willing to bite had done so, while others were on high alert, no longer inclined to bite a fake fly. Perhaps the nomads in the drift boat knew that fishing in a given Red Zone can be quickly and effectively covered, then it's time to immediately move on, knowing that changing the fly and method would probably prove fruitless. Better to move on and locate fresh willing fish than to linger and hope new fish will wander into the area, or that wary fish will finally lose their caution. This "hit and run" strategy was definitely working for them, and I could not help but appreciate how much work it is to drop anchor, make a few casts, start up the motor, move to a new spot, drop the anchor, and repeat the routine over and over. There is a natural inertia in most of us whereby we tend to stay in the same location too long after it is no longer productive. The Red Zone can is a moving target. Sometimes it travels very quickly. Discipline can be necessary.

When I think about heavily-fished popular lakes like Diamond Lake I wonder if the fish can actually be harder to catch. Here's my thinking, with the thousands of anglers who fish Diamond Lake in a year, tens of thousands of fish are killed, removed from the population. All the fish in the lake, I think, at one time or another are going to have the opportunity to eat something with a hook in it and be thrown into the cooler. Those trout that have a higher degree of wariness have a greater chance of surviving. So, the pool of fish that remain for we fly-anglers to catch may very well contain a high number of cautious, not-easily-fooled individuals. To create more wary fish, or enhance the wariness of those already cautious, many or most fly-anglers release some or all of their catch. Inadvertently we may have "educated" these released fish so that they are reluctant to bite anything that might have a hook in it. Also, for those "educated" fish that *are* willing to bite, perhaps they are quicker to enter a cautious no-bite mode when disturbed. They are hyper vigilant.

In light of the speculative case I have just made, the hit-and-run strategy seems to fit well. Quickly and thoroughly cover the water in your immediate vicinity, and then move on in an attempt to discover undisturbed fish. And, this may be especially pertinent in areas where the water is shallow, let's say less than ten feet. Chuck and I and the nomads were in water typically 6 – 7 feet deep. There is no immediate retreat to deep water in this area when danger comes. It is reasonable that fish will go on high alert when fishing and boating activities are so close overhead.

More Red Zone Thoughts

On Day 2 Chuck and I had fair to good fishing on Diamond Lake with Chironomid pupae before a strong persistent wind caused us to end our day early.

Day 3 we launched about 8 a.m. We anchored in a location that had produced well for us the last two days. During the first 45 minutes we had no strikes, and did not spot any fish cruising the shallow water in which we were sitting, as we had the previous two days. Were we too early?

Soon a motorized boat cruised near our position and anchored two long casts north of us. The pilot knew exactly where he wanted to be. He made a good call. Within his first few casts, as he stripped in his artificial in small, short spurts, he was into a fish. Soon he was into another, and another. Most irritating, especially because he wanted to make sure that everyone within shouting distance knew he had *another* trout on his line.

Always an interesting combination: big fish, little fly. It's a Pheasant Tail Chironomid Pupa.

Neither of us had gotten strike one during the antics of the carnival barker, so I finally switched over to a rod with my clear, slow-sinking fly line and a Flashback Hare's Ear nymph. There were a few *Callibaetis* mayflies on the water, so it seemed like a good fly to start with. As usual, I mirrored the annoying angler's cast and retrieve. Nothing. So, I changed flies and repeated the process, spraying the casts in all directions. I eventually tried ten different nymphs and leeches. Nothing. Chuck had coaxed one Chironomid strike during my experimentation.

It was definitely time to move our boat. When the anchor was dropped again we were about a hundred feet west of Whoopi, careful not to settle too close to his casting zone. I can be annoyed without being inconsiderate.

Once settled in I could observe fish cruising all around us in about seven feet of water. We had found the fish, but could we get them to bite. We both opted to dangle Chironomids. Watching the fish swim near our flies, our hopes were high. Fifteen minutes elapsed. Nothing. I needed to change something, so I moved to the other side of the boat and cast my Chironomids directly in Whoopi's direction. My flies landed far short of

his casts, so there was absolutely no encroachment into his personal fishing space.

My first five casts resulted in four hooked fish! I resisted the impulse to go rudely vocal in my success. For whatever reason, Whoopi's rod had gone cold. Chuck and I had some consistent action for about an hour. I would occasionally cast in a spectrum of directions, getting a very occasional strike in any direction other than directly at Whoopi. We never changed from the suspended Chironomid technique, even though the guys in the boat near us had had good success casting and stripping a fly, just as the Nomads two days earlier. It wasn't too long after our new-found success began, the Whoopster and his friend headed for some distant location, never to be seen by us the rest of the day.

The events of the morning further solidified my understanding that productive Red Zones can be very localized. Though we could watch fish cruising all around us, it was obviously no guarantee that we could get them to bite. Perhaps they were merely passing by to get to the Red Zone, where they would settle in, lingering to dine in a very specific location. At least for awhile. Red Zones move, and so must we anglers. Locating the fish will always be Job One.

Communication Network

There is one more excellent fish-searching tool at my disposal when I fish with friends. We can all spread out a bit and conduct independent searches. When anyone in the posse discovers something of interest, the info is shared. If we are all in the same general area, good news can be dispensed by speaking up. When distances between us are great or we choose not attract unwanted attention, we have an additional way to communicate . . . .

One summer day as I was almost ready to launch my boat on Big Lava Lake in the Oregon Cascades I met John and Suzie Schultz. They drove up to my launch site to survey the scene, to eventually put onto the lake themselves. From Idaho, it was their first trip to Lava. As we chatted they told me they were meeting some fishing friends who would join them a little later in the day.

John Schultz is fully armed and loaded on Lava Lake, OR — electric motor, depth finder/fish locator, multiple rods, and a two-way radio over his heart.

A few hours later I encountered John on the lake. As we traded information about the morning's fishing, I was able to see how John had "tricked out" his pontoon boat. Besides the standard fishing equipment onboard, he was set up with an electric motor and battery pack, a depth finder/fish locator, and a two-way radio secured near his left breast shirt pocket. He was the ultimate fly-fishing combination of propulsion, electronic information gathering, and communication. Our conversation ended when a radio message came in from one of his fishing friends on the lake indicated they had found the

fish and John should join them. Ten four, copy that, over and out. Fish on!

Inexpensive "walkie talkie" radios are very useful. Cell phones can work, too, but provider service in many of the quality lake locations in my state is quite sketchy. Two-way radios work every time . . . if you remember to use *charged* batteries. Carry spares! Every successful stillwater fly-fishing assassin has a checklist. Batteries are on it.

I Reiterate

I may have located and caught fish for a time on my lake of the day, but this is an ephemeral event. In a matter of minutes or hours, the bite will end in my immediate area. Several possibilities must be considered. Perhaps the aquatic insects that drew fish to this particular location have ceased their hatching activity, so the fish are moving elsewhere. If the water is relatively shallow, sunlight intensity or fishing activity have moved the fish out of the area. Maybe the fish in my current zone are sated; they have eaten their fill and it's siesta time. Whatever the reason, it's time for me to track down another location where I can find a concentration of willing fish. I am always driven by the assumption that somewhere on the lake biting fish await me, IF I can find them. It's like a treasure hunt. I gather information; I make a reasonable guess, and then move my boat in that direction, again using my visual, electronic, and trolling tools. If I have a fly-fishing posse with me using the same tools, we WILL find the fish.

Beware the Traps

Fish hunting and locating form the cornerstone of a successful trip. These are not haphazard endeavors. The pursuit should be thoughtfully planned, systematic, and methodical.

Trap #1: Some days the fish are foolish and suicidal. These are the times that lull an inexperienced or lazy angler into believing he is a killer lake fisherman with mad stillwater fly-fishing skills. Usually sooner than later, those with a casual approach to locating fish on a lake will have poor fish-catching results.

Trap #2: The obvious prognosis that an inexperienced or non-cerebral angler will make when the fishing is poor is that the fish are not biting, not in the mood. This may or may not be true. Experienced, intelligent stillwater anglers continue to search when a Red Zone area isn't found quickly, and seek out a new Hot Spot when the fishing-catching fades. And, they smartly use all the fish-finding tools and strategies I have just discussed here. Remember the Nomads.

TEN

Stillwater Nymphs All-Star Team

W hen I fish lakes and ponds I take an athletic duffle bag with more than two dozen fly boxes! Effective stillwater fly-fishing can be very fly-intensive, much, much more so than angling moving waters. In large part I attribute this to the fact that in an environment without currents to move and somewhat distort the viewing of the fly, an interested trout has the opportunity to closely examine a nymph before it decides to eat it. Even the *shade* of a particular color of a fly can be crucial. I could put twice as many members on my stillwater All-Star team as are featured below. Instead I have selected the best of the best.

The **Pheasant Tail Nymph** (image to the right) is an excellent immature mayfly imitation. When *Callibaetis* mayfly nymphs are swimming to the surface to transform into adults the PT is a good choice. Adjusting the hook size and pinching off the tail, I have a very reasonable Chironomid pupa. The hairy pheasant tail fibers and the peacock thorax make for an enticing combination for trout and char. A bead head and/or flashback can be added as a variation on a theme. Sizes 12 – 20.

Not much of a "looker", the **Skinny Minnie** (image next page top left) is a surprisingly effective fly, fished with a slow troll, with a cast-and-retrieve method, or suspended under an indicator. It confounds me at times when Chironomids are the fish menu item of choice how the Minnie will be taken before a much more realistic Chironomid fly. It doesn't always play out this way, but often enough to make me marvel at this simpleton assassin. The combination of thin profile, peacock herl, and short gray partridge hackle is a winner. Sizes 10 – 16.

I cannot argue with this fly's longevity. The **Gold Ribbed Hare's Ear** has been around for a century and a half, and still makes many nymph anglers' Top Ten list. Though often tied with a metal bead at the head, my preference is most often bead-free. A strip of flat pearl mylar over the body and/or thorax, and a pair of pearl Krystal Flash legs, may add sex appeal for some fish. Sizes 10 – 20.

If I had only one fly to fish the rest of my life for any freshwater species . . . make mine a **Prince Nymph**. With its brown biot tails and white biot "wings", and iridescent peacock body, this fly doesn't resemble any aquatic insect I have seen, but fish everywhere — lake or river — want to eat it. I carry both bead-head and standard ties. Sizes 10 – 16.

More peacock, please. I have created numerous effective patterns inspired by my success with the **Skinny Minnie**. When dragonfly nymphs are active, the Skinny Minnie Dragon can be deadly. I fish it with a pulsating, darting retrieve to imitate the natural swimming motion of the dragonfly nymph. It is also an excellent searching pattern when trolled slowly, and occasional twitches of the fly rod further activate the nymph. Sizes 8 – 12.

My good friend Matt Ramsey showed me this fly on a summer steelhead expedition, and he demonstrated that steelhead would, indeed, eat it. The **Hare Scud** is designed like a scud fly, a very common stillwater food source. It's quite effective anywhere "freshwater shrimp" are found. The Hare Scud is another simple fly with spiky hare's ear fur appeal. Readily-available dyed hare's ear dubbing fur allows for matching most real-life shades of olive, gray, gold, and tan. Sizes 10 – 14.

Another fishing friend, Rick Coxen, shared his **Goat Damsel** with me back in the early 1980's on Oregon's Crane Prairie Reservoir. When the damselfly nymphs were swimming for high ground, it felt a little bit like cheating using this pattern. It's a simple fly: Angora goat fur overlain with a few pheasant tail fibers, pheasant tail beard, and gold wire spiraled over the body for segmentation and security, and I want the fly thin. I vary the size and color, add water, then, fish it with confidence. The damsel nymph has a very distinctive swimming motion. Three short, medium slow strips of the line, followed by a three-count pause. Repeat. Sizes 10 – 14.

In keeping with the slender and peacock themes again, the **Skinny Minnie Damsel** nymph has proven itself to be a fly worthy of my stillwater All-Star Team. It certainly doesn't match the color scheme of most living damsel nymphs, so maybe there are trout seeking out the oddballs. I may change the color of the marabou tail, but all other materials remain the same. I will pair this pattern with my Goat Damsel on the leader, and the fish have two delectable choices. Sizes 10 – 14.

Cal Bird's **Bird's Nest** is simple and versatile. When caddis pupae are active or *Callibaetis* mayflies are hatching, the Bird excels. For surface-feeding trout on patrol

I cast this fly to the rise and initiate a very slow retrieve with good results. I use an un-weighted pattern in this situation. Pairing this fly with a cripple or dry fly on the dropper is particularly dangerous . . . in a good sort of way. Or, I may fish the Bird's Nest with a Hare's Ear, Pheasant Tail, or Epoxyback Callibaetis. Sizes 12 – 16.

Selective trout may demand a more realistic looking *Callibaetis* mayfly nymph, and this *the* fly. I will swim an **Poxyback Callibaetis** slowly in the surface on a floating line, or troll it deep on a full-sinker. I like it a lot for dangle nymphing. Removing the tail gives me a very passable Chironomid pupa. And, wouldn't I know, the PC has hare's ear fur and pheasant tail in its design. This is a hard-working All-Star, season after year . . . after season . . . after season. Sizes 12 – 16.

As I was teaching my sister Joann how to tie this killer midge pupa she persisted in referring to these flies as the pattern with a "gill hat". The comical name stuck. With endless mix-and-match options, I can fill an entire fly box with **Gill Hat Chironomids**, of a variety of body thread colors, wires, and bead finishes. However, all have a white Antron gill hat imitating pupal breathing filaments. The body of this fly is slim, slim, slim, just like the naturals. A red butt section can sometimes be the ticket for selective fish. Crazy effective fished under an indicator, or fished "naked". Sizes 10 – 20.

In lakes and ponds the **San Juan (Worm) Plus** is an imitation of those Chironomid larvae which have a hemoglobin-like substance which gives them their characteristic blood red color. They live in the silt and detritus of the bottom, where trout cruise to find them. It's not always necessary, but tying the Plus with a small-diameter red Vernille can enhance the enticement of the smaller sizes. I hang it just off the bottom under an indicator. Sizes 10 – 18.

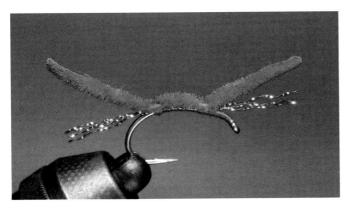

This pattern specifically emulates the shimmering grayish-tan body color of a Chironomid pupa swelled and changed by gasses trapped underneath the skin. The sheen of the **Gunmetal Chironomid's** Flashabou body and its silvery color can be key visual triggers when the fish are being selective as they feed on ascending midge pupae. Anti-static bag material wrapped over gray or tan thread can also be used to also simulate the sheen and desired color. I prefer black or white beads, and a ribbing of copper, orange, or red. Sizes 10 – 18.

fishing naked, or suspended beneath an indicator, here's another simple-design All-Star. Sizes 12 – 16.

My final stillwater All-Star is the most unique. The **Horizontal Damsel Nymph** is meant to be fished under an indicator. When damselfly nymphs migrate at hatching time they are horizontally oriented as they swim in spurts to eventually crawl out of the water onto assorted vegetation, partially submerged wood, or rocks. During their swim, they pause frequently, hanging in the water column. I often fish this fly nearer the surface than the bottom; the insects finish their travels within a few feet or inches from the surface. After the nymph has been stationary for 15 – 20 seconds I pull the line very slowly for about a foot, then let it rest again. Sizes 10 – 14.

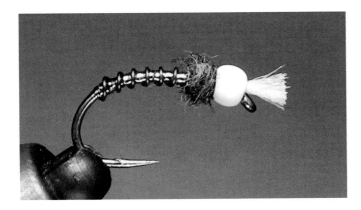

The **LaLaLa** (Larva Lace Larva) is a Chironomid bloodworm imitation, inspired by a simple fly shared with me by a former OSU student of mine, Patrick Allen. The hollow, soft-plastic tubing is slipped over the hook. The appearance is vivid transparent red, just like living bloodworms. I add a pinch of red synthetic dubbing fur to finish the fly at the head. Crept slowly

ELEVEN

Effective Stillwater Nymphing Techniques

There are three general stillwater nymph fishing methods, and a myriad of hybrids of these. Trolling, the cast-and-retrieve, and suspending a nymph in the water column are the bedrock techniques. Some days the fish can be caught with any of them; on others only one specific technique, or one specific hybrid, will entice the fish. A successful lake or pond nympher must become skilled at all these methods, and be willing to experiment until the day's fishing puzzle is solved.

Which Fly Line?

A floating fly line is the only choice for fishing nymphs, larvae, and pupae under a strike indicator on lakes and ponds, and casting-and-retrieving these flies in shallow water. As the fly lines for trolling and cast-and-retrieve methods, I will use one of four fly lines, the choice usually driven by the water depth or where in the water column the fish will take a fly. As for the latter, if the fish are concentrated over water fifteen feet deep but feeding on emerging nymphs or pupae at the surface, I will opt for a floating fly line, of course.

I have a minimum of two rods strung with hi-vis floating fly lines when fishing stillwaters. I need a floater for indicator fishing, casting and retrieving nymphs and pupae, and pitching dry flies and emergers.

I always have three or four strung rods with me when fishing lakes or ponds. For ease of pick up and casting I always prefer a floating fly line if the fish will allow me. Without any rise activity on a lake when I first arise I know my best bet is a sinking fly line. The slow-sinking or intermediate "transparent" line is the most versatile choice. I can fish shallow water without my flies immediately sinking into the mud or dragging through and fouling on the bottom vegetation. If I do fish it in deeper water, say 15 – 25 feet, I can cast it, wait a counted number of seconds, then retrieve or troll my flies.

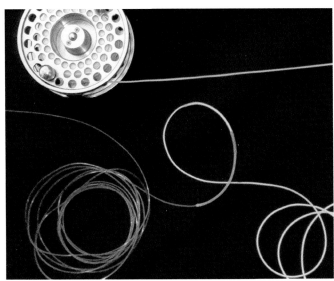

The floating portion of my clear sink-tip acts as an elongated strike indicator and makes the fly line much easier to pick up off the water for the re-cast.

If I consistently fish deep water, 15 – 30 feet for hours, then I will fish a Type III fly line. Unless the fish are cruising high in the water column, I want my nymphs to get deep quickly. This line buys more fishing time in deep water.

WF-6-S
TYPE III
2.50 - 3.50 ips
90 ft / 27 m

A Type III full-sinker is another "must" fly line in my arsenal.

If the fish are in shallow water, or feeding near the surface and the wind is blowing, a 15-foot clear sink-tip works best. In the wind the entirety of the floating fly line is blown into a sweeping arc, putting me out of straight-line contact with my flies and the fish. If a strike is soft, I may not know my fly was intercepted. If I

A clear intermediate is my most versatile full-sinking fly line.

do detect the strike I may not get a solid hook-up as I try to pull the line straight and tight against the fish. I do understand that the line is fairly tight even though it is in a large curve on the surface, but it does translate into more missed strikes compared to a straight-line configuration to my flies. The clear tip sinks below the surface currents created by the wind, and the shorter section of the bright-colored floating line acts as an elongated strike indicator, with the most distant portion of it progressively sunk because the sinking tip has pulled it under the surface. This line serves as a nice compromise when I want minimal sinkability when the wind blows, and the added strike-detecting feature and bester castability of the floating portion of the line.

Rod Tip Position
No matter which stillwater methods used I want my rod tip almost in the water. I seek to minimize the amount of slack line between the rod tip and the flies. This gives me the best chance to detect a subtle strike and immediately tighten the line to set the hook. When the rod tip is held high the slack line between the rod tip and the water dampens or absorbs a soft take of the fly, and the slack line must be tightened before the hook-set is secured, delaying the time between strike and set. This delay can be enough to allow the perp to escape.

Effective Trolling
When it comes to multi-tasking — visually searching for fish, watching other anglers, looking at the electronics screen, listening for helpful information, all while fishing — trolling is a super nymphing technique. It is the logical starting point once my boat is launched on most of

To minimize the possibility of a break-off on a hard strike, no fingers or hands on the reel or fly line. Rely on the reel's drag.

my fishing days. Even if I know I am headed to a distant point on the lake to concentrate my fishing efforts, I will troll my flies to get there.

This most basic of stillwater nymphing methods is a matter of stripping line from the reel, slowly moving the boat, and letting the flies trail behind it at a reasonable distance. Because the line is tight the strike will be felt when a fish intercepts the fly. Then, lift the rod tip to set the hook, play the fish, and lead it to the net. Sounds simple. However . . .

To troll effectively, there are technique variables which must be understood and attended to. Some of these variables include, extended fly line length behind the boat, the depth at which the flies are fished, the speed at which the flies are trolled, and the directional path of the flies. Discovering the right trolling nuances for the day assumes, of course, that I have made a wise fly choice, and the flies are being fished in a specific zone that actually has fish in it.

Hands (and Fingers) Off!

We all have tendencies and habits that are counterproductive to our fly-fishing success. One that I attempt to de-program in my students and clients is holding the fly line with the non-casting hand or pinning it against the cork as they troll. There are a couple of downside possibilities. First, a hard strike combined with a ham-handed hook-set can break off the fly. Secondly, a hard hook-set can actually tear a hook out of the fish's jaw if it is "lightly" secured in soft tissue or the membrane at the mouth's edge.

A reel with a good drag can be precisely set to do all the right work for securely setting the hook in the fish's

jaw and cushioning the impact of a hard strike or an overly enthusiastic hook-set. The correct drag setting is one where there is sufficient resistance to bury the hook point in the jaw when the rod tip is lifted, while at the same time a bit of line is pulled from the reel on this impact, cushioning the force like a shock absorber. This is a very important concept when light tippets and small flies are needed to catch trophy fish.

Trolling Error

Assuming my fly choice is good, and there are fish in the area being trolled, the most basic of errors I have made, and observe others make, is moving too fast. Real-life aquatic insects are tiny creatures. Even at high speeds for their size, small aquatic bugs cannot cover much distance.

Let's pretend we are dealing with a mobile underwater bug which is 1/2-inch long. If our little friend is pulled through the water at the rate of one foot per second, which is not a fast pace for you and me as we troll, this is 24 insect body lengths "swum" in one second. Let's try to understand if this is a reasonable insect swimming speed commonly seen by the fish that eat them on a regular basis.

Olympic swimming gold medalist Michael Phelps holds the 100-meter butterfly-stroke world record at 49.82 seconds, which is an average speed of about 4.49 (~4.5) mph.

Callibaetis *nymphs are good swimmers, but they don't normally cruise at the insect equivalent of 100 miles per hour.*

Michael Phelps is 6' 4" tall, or 76 inches, 152 times the length of our 1/2-inch swimming insect.

100 meters is 3937 inches. 3937" divided by 76" = 51.8 Michael Phelps body lengths. Let's say 52 body lengths for round numbers. So, to complete his 100-meter race, Mr. Phelps must swim a distance of 52 body lengths.

At an average speed of about 4.5 mph over a distance of 100 meters in 49.82 (~50) seconds, Michael Phelps is

Experiment with the trolling line length. Once a fish is caught the astute angler knows exactly the length that caught the fish in order to repeat this detail.

swimming at just over 1 body length per second for a world-record time. Our 1/2-inch swimming insect being trolled through the water at 12 inches (24 body lengths) per second is traveling at the human swimming equivalent of 4.5 mph X 24 body lengths — 108 mph!

For me, the single most important element of effective trolling is to go s-l-o-w-l-y. This has to be a conscious effort since my natural tendency is to focus on other fish-searching elements as I troll. Suddenly I realize I am moving too quickly. Also, after missing a couple of strikes my natural anxious inclination is to "hurry up" to get another strike. I must fight this tendency again. I must remind myself:

With flies in tow
Those "in the know"
Troll their nymphs slow.

Not only do I attempt to go slowly, I punctuate my trolling with periodic stops. As I come to a halt my flies descend. As I begin to move again my flies rise a bit in the water column. There are times that the descent or the ascent of my nymphs will prompt a strike. When I get a grab I make note of what my fly was doing — trolling speed, or paused, ascending, descending, or holding

steady. Additionally, I make note of the water depth, and my exact location in relationship to specific landmarks, such as a point, a bay, a stream, a tree, a campsite, an island, and such. How far am I from a nearby shoreline? A long cast? Two long casts? As far as I can throw a baseball? Perhaps I want to revisit this location, especially if I get multiple strikes, so my exact location is important. If I am far removed from the shore I may record my coordinates into my GPS device.

Trolling Line Length

Another very important detail about trolling effectively is to know the exact line length. My standard line measure is a pulled line "strip": grasping the fly line at the fly reel I pull the line to the first rod guide. This is one strip. Thirteen being my favorite number for many reasons, I often start trolling by putting out 13 strips of line. Depending on the conditions, I may eventually strip more line from the reel if I don't get any results with the initial 13. Once I discover the line length that gets me strikes, I always return to that length after reeling in the fish. This is another important detail I am very careful not to overlook.

Fishing always seems better when there is a breeze to riffle the lake's surface. It limits the fishes' above-surface vision a bit, and gives them a sense of protection from airborne predators. When the lake is flat and the sun is high, fishing can be very challenging. I must extend the length of line I am trolling to put greater distance between the disturbance of my movement and my flies. In the extreme, I may need to strip out my entire fly line, a length to 90' – 100'. I may also need to increase my leader length to create more distance between my visible fly line and my nymphs. Such adjustments can very well be the difference between catching fish and getting skunked.

Zigging and Zagging

It's easy to envision that fish will scatter in shallow water when I run my boat over them. This can be particularly important when the lake is windless. I have had good trolling success when fishing is difficult by deviating from trolling in a straight-line path. I will start trolling as if I am driving a broad obstacle course. Scribing an "S" or tracking the number 8 with my boat as I troll prevents my fly line from traveling directly through the exact zone where I may have disturbed the fish. And, not only is the line off to one side or the other of the water over which my boat has just floated, but the fly speed changes, and rises and drops in the water column, as I go into a turn or come out of a turn. As before, when I get a strike I make note of what was going on with the boat, my line, and my flies when the strike came. There may be a pattern which I need to discern and repeat.

Don't Be a One-Trick Pony

Back in my fly-fishing shop retail days, I had a customer who had a friend who had recently introduced him to fly-fishing lakes. Occasionally he would show me photos of a trophy rainbow he had recently caught. His success fueled his passion, so spring and summer he dedicated much of his spare time to pursuing fish in lakes. No mention ever of fishing streams or rivers.

I had another customer whom I took from a Ground Zero beginner into a good stream angler. Because he knew the lake angler just mentioned, Mr. Stream Angler invited Mr. Lake Angler on a guided fishing river trip with a guide outside my personal guiding area. After their fishing trip, Mr. Stream confided in me how the day started on their adventure together.

As the guided trip began the guide instructed Mr. Stream and Mr. Lake to cast to likely spots from his moving boat. Mr. Lake was in trouble. His attempts to cast

"He's a one-trick pony . . . But he turns that trick with pride." Lyrics by Paul Simon. Photo by BLM.gov.

a fly line were futile. Line and leader were everywhere except where they needed to be. It seems that Mr. Lake, though he had been fly-fishing for a few years now, had never actually cast a fly line. Though fishing lakes successfully, he had always merely stripped line from his fly line from his reel, letting it extend out behind his moving pontoon boat. After reeling in a fish, the trolling resumed again by pulling line from the reel and letting his boat movement straighten the line, never casting it. Mr. Lake was essentially a one-trick pony, limiting himself to a single stillwater method.

Frankentroll

An effective trolling hybrid technique involves adding a short line pull and release, a slow retrieve which continually shortens the line length, or slow hand-twist retrieve. The last two possibilities are executed when the boat is stopped after trolling a short distance, while the first is done with the boat on the move.

The first hybrid starts with a slow troll during which short pulls of the fly line, 2 – 4 inches, are made. The fly line is not actually retrieved and held, but pulled and, then, released again. To the fish the fly is seen moving laterally through the water, and then it darts ahead a few inches, and then returns to its steady swimming rate. Dart – steady, steady, steady – dart – steady, steady, steady . . . When done properly, even when the nymph darts ahead, it has only accelerated a little, and only a few inches. When it doubt, go slower, not faster.

A second Frankentroll technique intersperses a slow troll for a short distance (perhaps a rod length), a stopping of the boat, followed by stripping in 6' – 10' of fly line in little slow increments. The length of the retrieving strips and how quickly the line is pulled involve some experimentation. I suggest starting with 2- – 4-inch slow strips. Keeping the strip length the same, experiment next with a somewhat faster pull after the next short troll and stop. Vary the pause time between strips. Finally, experiment with longer line strips, again trying different pause times and the speed of the line strips. During all these stops and starts, once I have resumed the troll portion of the technique I lower the rod tip to the water, shake the tip back and forth quickly, and allow the slack line I have stripped onto my lap to extend the line fully behind the boat again. No need to re-cast until I change techniques or reel in to row the boat to a new location.

Franken #3 combines a short-distance troll & stop with a slow, steady hand-twist retrieve of the flies. A hand-twist involves grasping the fly line 6 – 8 inches in front of the fly reel with the thumb and first finger. The other three fingers are placed on top of the line away from the angler, then the three together sweep the line under the thumb and first finger back toward the angler. Once swept back, the three fingers hold the line steady against the palm while the thumb and first finger reach forward again to grasp the line and start the movement all over again. As with most fly retrieves, this is a very slow movement. Sometimes painfully slow. Patience will pay off. Done effectively, I often feel that my hand-twist retrieve is merely keeping the slack out of the line while the flies slowly sink. Once I have retrieved 6 – 10 feet of fly line, I begin the troll, shaking out the slack fly line as I swish the rod tip back and forth.

Crazy Town Retrieve

Shortly after I have made a strong case for fishing nymphs and pupae very slowly in stillwaters, I am going to relate a story which highlights an exception to my rule. It starts with an accidental discovery born of frustration.

Eastern Washington State has some great trout lakes. During my fly-shop retail days we always had an annual event fishing desert lakes between Vantage and Coulee City. A very popular one I fished many times is Lake Lenice.

Certain fishing friends of mine are very competitive; fish counts matter. The challenge was on one spring day as about a dozen of us fished Lenice. There was lots of pride at stake. I was determined to claim the high rod honors. Pride before the fall . . . perhaps.

The bite was slow. Everyone, including me, had landed but a few fish during the entire morning session. Early afternoon I left the main body of the lake to position my pontoon boat at the edge of a broad channel bounded by

Oregon and Washington's quality high-desert lakes can produce spectacular trout fishing.

an island on one side and the main shore of the lake on the other. I turned so that the high sun was at my back, providing excellent visibility into the depths. I watched cruising rainbow trout patrolling back and forth in the channel. It was entertaining and informative to watch the fish as I presented a variety of nymphs fished with a variety of methods to the cruisers. They were obviously on the move looking for something to eat, but none of my trick flies fished with dependable techniques interested the finicky rainbows.

I watched in disbelief as fish after fish ignored my beloved size-14 Prince Nymph as it swam, hesitated, ascended, descended, or jigged near the trout. So in frustration I decided to change flies again. I started rip-stripping the Prince back at high speed to hurry the changing of the guard. As the fly screamed in my direction a 14-inch rainbow grabbed it hard. WTH? A bizarre anomaly, I thought, until another fish slammed the Prince again!

After a few more landed trout I hit the main lake again to share (brag about?) my good fortune with my colleagues. On the way I experimented with a combination of high-speed trolling with a stripping retrieve of the Prince. Wham! Fish on. And another. By the time I found my friends I had landed eleven fish with my high-velocity rip & strip. After landing a few more fish the bite died. And I have never experienced success with this "lucky accident" technique ever again.

Oh, yes. That day on Lake Lenice I was high rod — by far.

Artful Science

Trolling is a precise art; a scientific art. It is an effective technique with variations the angler paints himself as he develops a "feel" for the right combination of the

Lenice, Nunnaly, Dry Falls, and Lenore lakes in eastern Washington are stillwaters to put on your list.

variables. To execute trolling and its nuanced variations effectively details must be noted. Look for patterns that may lead to success on the lake today and experiment thoughtfully until you find them.

Cast-and-Retrieve Methods

There are times when trolling flies or suspending them under an indicator work well, but I will put these methods aside to cast and retrieve a fly. This technique has two attractive elements for me: it's proactive (versus passive) involvement with the rod, the line, and manipulation of the flies, and secondly, I like the surprise tug of a fish as it hits the fly. If the fishing has been good, and I am somewhat sated, the method becomes more important than bolstering my fish numbers.

Once the cast is made, and the flies allowed to settle and sink a bit, I have many options, many variables to tend to which will have a bearing on my fishing success or failure. How long should I let the fly sink before I begin my retrieve? Will I strip the line to move the fly or will I use a hand-twist retrieve? If I strip line, what is the length of my line strip/pull? Are all strips the same length or do I vary them? How quickly or slowly should I pull the line? How long do I pause between line strips, it at all?

I have a simple retrieving guideline to follow if imitating a specific insect. If I am familiar with how a given nymph or pupa swims I want to mimic its swimming movements. For instance, a dragonfly swims in pulsing bursts. For retrieving the artificial, I make 6 – 10 short, medium-speed pulls on the fly line, and then pause for a count of three. If you want to see a dragonfly nymph swimming check out YouTube.

Another example of distinctive swimming movement is that of the damselfly nymph. When these insects are migrating through the water to reach the shore or an exposed rock, log, or cattails on which to crawl out of the water to hatch into the adult stage, their swimming movement can be readily observed. They wiggle quickly laterally, swishing their abdomens side to side to propel them forward. They do not swim as fast as a dragonfly so I retrieve the damselfly nymph a bit slower, but with the same 6 – 10 short line pulls interspersed with a three-count pause.

If I cast and retrieve a Chironomid pupa I will use a very slow hand-twist retrieve. Essentially all I am doing is keeping the line tight. The pupa can wiggle a bit but it does not swim. To put more movement on this type of fly can definitely be unconvincing to the fish. A little knowledge of aquatic entomology can pay big dividends for accurately and effectively retrieving nymphs and pupae.

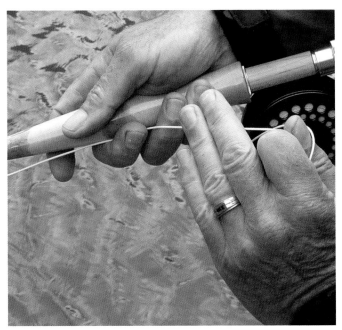

The hand-twist retrieve is a good counter to the tendency to retrieve a nymph too quickly. It can be productive to intersperse pauses of a few seconds into this retrieve.

For non-specific patterns that don't closely imitate a particular insect, such as the Prince Nymph, there are broad ranges of retrieving variables with which to experiment. I tend to start out fishing such flies with short, slow strips of the line, interspersed with pauses. It's interesting how often fish will intercept a fly when it is in pause mode. Of course the fly is not totally stationary; it's sinking. Because the interception of a "stationary" fly can be quite subtle, the best chance of detecting the fish is when fishing a hi-vis floating fly line, or a clear sink-tip fly line with a bright yellow floating body. I watch the farthest point of the floating line. The floating line is never perfectly straight on the water; there are always little "S" curves in it. If I see the slightest straightening of the most distant "S" I set the hook. If an angler does not know to look for this he will never know a fish bit the fly. Typically, there will be less than a second to see the strike and set the hook.

A Crane-bow Story

One of the premiere trophy trout lakes in Oregon is Crane Prairie Reservoir in the Oregon Cascades, south of Bend. The large rainbow trout there have a local nickname: Crane-bow. I was fishing the damselfly nymph migration on a late-June day. Because the water I was fishing was less than 10 feet deep I chose to fish my clear sink-tip. I had tied on a trusty Goat Damsel, and casted perhaps 25 feet from my float tube. Though I was talking to one of my fishing companions at the time of this particular

The Goat Damsel. Yummy.

cast, I knew from experience not to take my eyes off the line as it settled to the surface and the nymph began to sink. My plan was to wait for a count of ten, then begin retrieving the fly.

About half way through my silent countdown I saw the most distant little "S" in the floating portion of my fly line straighten slightly. If I had not focused specifically at the far end of the floating line I never would have known a trout had picked up the descending damsel. Certainly the strike would never have been felt.

Oregon's Crane Prairie Reservoir was a wooded mountain meadow dammed and flooded in the 1920's. Big rainbow trout live here.

A chunky cranebow. (Crane/Rainbow)

When I lifted the rod tip I came tight against a quality fish. When I finally brought it to hand and released it, I estimated its weight at seven pounds.

Dangle Nymphing

There are times when fish will definitely prefer a nymph or pupa as it ascends toward the surface. This preference is usually revealed when the fly line and leader have been retrieved to the point that it's time to re-cast. Experience has taught me to lift the line slowly from the water on the off chance a fish is following and may grab the fly just before it is pulled out of the water. I wish I had a nickel for every time a fish smacks my fly as I begin to lift the line to begin another cast. When I hook a fish in this instance, an observer will think I was actually setting the hook, when — truth be told — it was a lucky accident.

In the journaling chapter I relate using this dangle nymphing quite effectively at Oregon's East Lake during a long weekend when the trout and kokanee exhibited a very prominent preference for a nymph hanging straight below the boat. There were numerous times when I had my rod propped against the gunwale of my drift boat, hands occupied with taking photos, searching one of my fly boxes, or dealing with aquatic insects I had captured. Suddenly the rod tip would start bouncing when a trout or salmon latched onto one of the flies as it merely hung there, sometimes only five or six feet below the surface.

Dangle nymphing starts with the line and nymphs directly below the rod tip.

Details of the Dangle

At first mention the technique sounds embarrassingly simple: the fly line and leader hang in the water straight down from the rod tip into the lake's depths directly beneath the boat. The flies are quietly suspended in a zone somewhere between a few inches off the bottom to a few feet below the surface. At times, dangle nymphing has the potential to out-fish all other stillwater methods for presenting nymphs, larvae, and pupae. However, it's the little attendant details and subtle manipulations of the flies with this technique which determine its degree of success. Because 6X and 7X tippets are sometimes required to fool large fish, I employ a peculiar retrieve of the line and use a specific rod action in order to prevent a break-off by a trophy trout. And, of course, fly selection and the correct arrangement of multiple artificials on the leader are critical elements of the success formula, too.

Pumping a fish's stomach offers a huge clue as to which nymphs to "dangle". Here, a vial full of* Callibaetis *nymphs.

With countless numbers of swimming *Callibaetis* mayfly nymphs available to the fish, I figured a slow and varied retrieve of the reliable size-14 Pheasant Tail Nymph or Bird's Nest on a sinking line would prove irresistible, as in past years at East Lake. Tiny Chironomid pupae are always available to hungry fish, too. So, suspending a size-18 – -22 midge pupa, paired with a Pheasant Tail, can account for many fish in my day's effort.

Essential Equipment

To decrease the possibility of a break-off on a hard strike or an overly enthusiastic hook-set, I use a light 3-weight fly rod with a forgiving, slow-action tip. I am seeking maximum forgiveness — *mea maxima culpa* — from a rod tip that will act as a springy shock absorber for a wispy 7X tippet. My hand and fingers never touch the line, risking too much resistance against a hard strike; I want the cushioning effect of a precise, lightly-set reel drag. Even with a

Feathering the reel spool is a safe way to retrieve the fly line in case a hard strike happens, especially when light tippets are a must.

gentle hook-set and the right rod I still lost four Chironomid pupae to trout on the strike in a couple of days.

A hand-stripping or hand-twist retrieve of the line to slowly bring the flies up through the water column is problematic. When the line is held tight while being retrieved upward, there may not be enough shock absorption when the fish grabs the fly. A soft rod tip may be insufficient by itself. So, another critical technique to decrease the chance of breaking off a good fish with dangle nymphing is a specialized retrieve of the line for additional cushioning of the strike and hook-set. For maximum effectiveness, this retrieve must be paired with a quality fly reel equipped a smooth, precision drag.

An obvious way to spool line onto the reel is to grasp the reel handle and crank it. However, there is no "give" when a strike comes. I want some line pulled *off* the spool to cushion the strike. So my solution is to retrieve the line slowly and intermittently by lightly feathering/turning the spool with my fingers on its edge. If a fish pulls hard the spool will spin to release line with minimal friction from my fingers. The reel drag must be set precisely so that line is released with minimal pull. However the drag cannot be set so lightly that I risk a line overrun. It's a delicate balance. A bit of trial and error is involved in finding the right setting.

My favorite fly line for this method in most situations is a Type III density-compensated sinking fly line. It gets my flies near the bottom with reasonable haste, but not so fast that they are dragging in the silty lake bottom if I choose to mix in the standard cast-and-retrieve with my dangling. A clear intermediate, slow-sinking line is preferable in water 12 feet deep or less, and may actually be preferable in deeper water when the fish are on high alert in extremely clear water. Fluorocarbon leaders and tippets are always my choice.

The Art of the Dangle Retrieve

I want to know the water depth. I usually have my electronic depth finder attached to the boat. If I'm in 20 feet of water, I don't need to cast more than 30 feet of line and leader. I experiment with a variety of retrieves, mixing a spectrum of retrieve lengths and speeds, interspersed with pauses, until the line is vertical directly below me. With an extremely light tippet, I prefer to retrieve line by turning the reel spool with my fingers on the spool's edge rather than stripping the line by hand, doing my best to avert a break-off. Once the line is vertical and the flies off the bottom, I will slowly raise the rod tip a foot or two, simulating an insect ascending toward the surface. Slow is critical. There is a natural tendency to move our flies much faster than real insects move through the water. There are many times that no retrieve, no movement is very effective.

This East Lake brown trout was "dangled" on a Flashback Pheasant Tail nymph.

After raising and lowering the rod tip, I may repeat the exact same movement again without turning the spool to retrieve any line. The slow ascent or descent of the flies can be a trigger for a fish on the hunt. If I get no response to the lift and drop I will slowly turn the reel spool with my fingers, expecting a strike at any time. After retrieving a foot or two of line onto the spool, I repeat the slow lift and drop of the rod tip again. I may pause the lift and drop for a count of ten, letting the flies hang motionless for a bit. I continue this routine until the upper end of the 9-foot leader breaks the surface. As I lift to recast, I do so slowly on the chance that a fish has followed the flies and may decide to strike as the flies are about to exit the water. This is not an unusual occurrence, especially in water with low visibility or low-light conditions.

My Favorite Dangle Flies

The Skinny Minnie, Bead Prince, Flashback Hare's Ear, Flashback Pheasant Tail, Bird's Nest, Gunmetal Chironomid, Plain Jane Chironomid, and Poxyback Callibaetis are dangle nymphing "must" flies for me, in a variety of sizes, of course.

The Poxyback Callibaetis is a deadly imitation of the Callibaetis ***mayfly nymph.***

The Leader Set-Up

Where legal, I always fish multiple flies. Two different flies give the fish a choice, and I have the two artificials suspended at different depths, one of which may have a fly close enough to entice a stillwater cruiser in the vicinity. For dangle nymphing a nine-foot tapered leader is usually adequate. I prefer one with a small-diameter butt section, typically 0.015" – 0.017". The smaller diameter allows for quicker, straight-line sinkability of the leader and flies. To create such a leader, trim off the upper 3 feet of a standard 9-foot tapered fluorocarbon leader, then add back tippet of the appropriate diameter. As an example, if I cut the butt section from a 9-foot 4X tapered leader, I can secure lengths of 5X, 6X, or 7X to it and have the completed leader cast reasonably well.

To splice on a dropper fly about 24 inches above the point fly, at about the 7-foot mark on the leader I either add two additional feet of tippet, or cut and rejoin the sections, using a double surgeon knot. When correctly tied, the surgeon knot will have a tag end that points up the leader toward the rod tip, while the second tag points away from the rod tip toward the point/terminal fly.

As I prepare to tie the knot I make sure that the tag pointing *toward* the point fly is about 3 inches long when the knot is pulled tight. I trim off the short tag pointing up the leader, then secure the dropper fly to the long tag. When tied in place the dropper fly will hang about 2 – 2 ½ inches from the main leader. The dropper line must be short to prevent tangling and twisting around the leader. I know of six different ways to tie or secure a dropper fly to a leader. In my opinion, the method I have described here is overwhelmingly

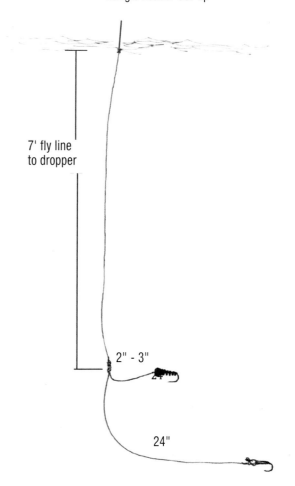

7' fly line to dropper

2" - 3"

24"

the best, and is superior to the popular (and temptingly easy) method of tying the final two feet of tippet to the bend of the hook of a fly clinch-knotted to the main leader at the 7-foot mark. My dropper fly swims or hangs more naturally, and the hook is in the best position to securely hook a fish as it hangs free, without the line blocking easy access to the full "bite" of the hook when the tippet is secured at the hook bend.

Dangle nymphing can be so simple it's easy to overlook as a viable method to catch stillwater species. After decades of lake and pond fishing I have learned to be patient, to fish my flies *slowly* all the way to the surface before re-casting. Once a few fish have revealed their preference for striking my fly as it ascends vertically, I will, then, focus more specifically on the dangle portion of my retrieve. A gentle lift and lowering of the rod tip can prompt savage strikes, so no hands or fingers on the fly line is imperative. For cushioned resistance, the strike should pull line from the reel spool with a precisely-set, light drag. The dangle is usually not a "stand alone" technique, but rather a complement, an add-on, to the more traditional cast-and-retrieve method. The fish have taught me to pay attention when my flies lift off the lake bottom, taught me that they can prefer my flies suspended and gently puppeteer-ed directly beneath my rod tip. As always, they lead the dance, and I learn to follow.

A Quick Review

The dangle technique begins with a short cast of Type III density-compensated sinking fly line, typically no more than 25 feet. I want my nymphs down and near the bottom reasonably quickly, and I want the line oriented more vertically than horizontally, thus the short cast. The deeper the water the longer the time my flies are in the vertical position as I slowly lift-and-drop and retrieve the fly line, s-l-o-w-l-y raising and lowering the rod tip a foot or so, occasionally finger-feathering my reel spool to reel in a bit of fly line.

1.Make a short cast and wait 10 – 15 seconds for the flies to sink.

2.Raise the rod tip *very* slowly for a foot or two, and, then, drop the tip back to the water.

3.As the rod tip is lowered into position for another lift, spin the reel spool with the fingertips to retrieve six or eight inches of fly line. I don't want to get caught with my hand on the reel handle because I might break the fish off when there is no line release from the spool as I set the hook.

4.Intersperse pauses with the lifts and drops. The strike may come when the flies are motionless. Remember: Chironomid pupae fished effectively under an indicator are motionless most of the time.

To prevent break-offs on the strike, the reel drag must be adjusted whereby there is enough resistance to bury the hook point on the set, but lightly enough that enough of the shock of the strike is cushioned.

A drift boat is a great vehicle to get friends — especially newbies like Scott and Carol Phenix — onto the lake.

Mirroring Success — Go to School

Because there are so many mix and match cast-and-retrieve combinations — strip length, strip speed, pauses, and pause length — there are challenging times when the puzzle solution cannot be easily discovered. I try many combinations of stripping and pausing the fly, but to no avail. So, if I can, I will seek out a "mentor", someone on the lake today who is having some success. It's time for me to go to school.

My friends and I had a memorable fish-catching day on Clark Canyon Reservoir one late July. The damselfly nymphs were migrating, and a slow troll of the flies produced great results on the hard-fighting rainbows. Day 2 was totally different.

I have often watched feeding fish cruise the shoreline. An anchor on a pontoon boat allows for fan-casting the shoreline from a fixed point.

The word was out. Our next day on the lake found us surrounded by many anglers trying their luck. We trolled as we had done the day before, with minimal results, only a very occasional strike, no fish landed. All anglers near us were experiencing the same. Something had changed. Time for school.

I separated myself from the herd in search of anyone who might actually be catching fish. Eventually I found him.

The successful angler in an inflatable pontoon boat with a fish bending his rod — again — was fishing by himself toward a corner of the reservoir. As is my custom, I moved to a position to his rear, and remained a considerable distance away. I could see a broad channel running between two weed beds, a likely place to cast my fly as I settled in to watch and fish. As usual, I deemed the location and retrieve more important than the fly. I stayed with my Goat Damsel nymph, readied to mirror his every movement. He would cast, and I would cast. He paused for a count of 10 or so to let the line sink, so I did the same. When he made two little line strips, I copied him. I watched him hook a fish, and within a minute I did the same. Here was the lesson again — be patient, integrate pauses into the retrieve, and don't hurry.

Indicator Fishing

One of the deadliest of all stillwater methods has risen to prominence in the last thirty years: suspending a fly underneath a strike indicator. Instead of taking the fly to the fish, the angler hopes a fish will come to the fly. A sunken nymph or pupa hangs in the water column to entice a cruising trout to eat it.

Aquatic plants like water lilies harbor food items and provide cover for hungry fish.

This method of fishing was brought to us from our British Columbia neighbors. The Canadians have been on the forefront of fine-tuning the equipment and Chironomid pupae fly patterns for indicator fishing. I have fished a broad variety of lakes in B.C, and virtually every angler I observe there relies on indicator fishing as their primary angling method, at least during the spring and early summer months. And, now it is a very popular stillwater technique adopted by American trout anglers.

The basic plan in indicator fishing is to suspend a fly about a foot or so off the bottom, assuming this is the primary cruising depth for trout looking for a snack. It is imperative, therefore, to know the exact depth of the water being fished. This is one of the reasons that every BC stillwater fly-fisher has an electronic depth finder on his boat.

Add a Little Movement

For us impatient sorts staring at a motionless strike indicator, waiting for it to signal a strike, can be a bit trying. We want to be doing something, be more actively engaged. So, if I don't get a strike in a minute or so I lift my rod tip a tiny bit to slowly move the indicator and flies about a foot. I reel in the bit of slack I have created, drop the rod tip to the water, and wait another minute before repeating these actions. It is common to prompt a fish to strike during this small repositioning of the flies, or immediately after the indicator settles into its new location. If the fish are definitely showing a preference for some movement in the suspended fly I will reposition it more often.

For those new to indicator fishing it is important to know that some strikes can be so gentle the strike indicator is disturbed very little. Rather than being pulled under water, sometimes I watch the indicator turn slightly, not even causing the water to ripple as it does so. If there is the slightest hint of indicator movement, set the hook. As I remind my guests, there are no penalty points for setting the hook, even when it's merely your imagination.

Though it happens many times that a little movement of the indicator flies will trigger a fish to bite, I am remembering a recent trip to East Lake as I write this. After three days of catching very good numbers of fish, my two largest fish of the trip — an 18-inch rainbow and a 17-inch brown trout — were caught as I fished a size-14 Flashback Pheasant Tail Nymph under an indicator. The fish showed absolutely no interest in a quiet, no-movement suspension of the fly. Strikes would come only as I drew the indicator a few feet toward me by lifting the rod tip. The fish took the fly as I initially started to move it, or in the midst of the lift.

No fly-fishing technique stands alone. There are always variations with which to experiment. Often, it is this variation or iteration that entices the fish to respond.

Deep-Water Indicator Fishing

When fishing ten feet of water or less an indicator can be secured at a fixed point on the leader, since the distance from the indicator to the point fly (remember I use two flies where legal) is no more than 9 feet. I use a popular thumbnail-size soft plastic bubble indicator. When a fish is brought to the net, lifting the rod high easily allows for having the indicator stay well away from the rod tip. When a distance of 20 feet between indicator and fly is necessary in deep water, a different type of indicator is necessary.

During one of my early visits to BC's Roche Lake there was a gathering of experienced anglers catching fish by suspending Chironomid pupae in 20 feet of water. I maneuvered in and around the group without trespassing on their fishing to confirm the water's depth. It was consistently 20 feet in the killing zone. There was no way my fixed plastic bubble indicator would work. Fortunately I had some foam slip strike models. With these, when the strike comes, the impact of the leader being pulled tight by the fish and the hook-set disengages the indicator so that it slides down the leader to the fly, or a stopper above the fly.

Additional Indicator Flies

Though stillwater indicator fishing was initially for suspending Chironomid pupae, some anglers experimented with suspending other flies to catch cruising fish. Small leeches, damselfly nymphs, dragonfly nymphs, Prince Nymphs, and members of the Skinny Minnie fly series can be deadly under an indicator. Some I will tie as "balanced" or horizontally-oriented patterns, which I include in Chapter 10: Stillwater Nymphs All-Star team on page 88.

My Horizontal Damsel is designed to suspend under an indicator, oriented horizontally like the real insect.

The Slow Lift

No matter what stillwater nymphing technique I employ, I have learned to pay attention for the possibility of a strike as I lift the line and leader to re-cast the flies. The enticement happens when the fly has gone from moving essentially horizontal to upwardly vertical. Fish have trained me over the years to anticipate a strike as I

prepare for the next cast. As detailed in Dangle Nymphing page 100, to enhance the possibility of inducing the strike on on a lift, I often pause half way through a lift, let the fly sink again, and then raise it up a second time before casting. The lift is just one more retrieve that can produce one more occasional fish during a fishing day.

Cast and Wait . . . and Wait Some More

I was fishing eastern Idaho's Henry's Lake in mid June. The strikes were sporadic fishing a Midnight Bugger and Prince Nymph, my standard pair of searching flies. Believing the lake's cutthroat and cuttbows could be caught if I discovered the right location and the right technique, I went on a search. I was determined to seek out anglers who were catching fish, observe where and how they were fishing. Boats were scattered over a broad area, but I finally spied an older gentleman sitting alone in his anchored pram, playing a fish. I circled around him in my float tube giving him wide berth, until I was positioned behind him. I did not want to throw him off his game if he knew I was watching him. In fact, there was a possibility he would quit fishing so as not to give nearby fishermen any clues about what he was doing to charm the fish.

After landing and admiring his fish, he made his next cast. The fly sailed about 40 feet before landing. I could not see the fly, of course, but it usually doesn't matter. Location and technique are often crucial. After the cast the man put his rod down, resting it on the stern of his boat. A smoker, he took several slow drags on this cigarette in a rather thoughtful manner. Then, he stripped his line a bit, reeled in the slack, and put his rod down again. He repeated this sequence of events a few times — and then he hooked another fish.

As for his chosen location, I discovered he was sitting over a broad deep hole. Rimming the expanse of deeper water was submerged vegetation, some of which grew almost to the surface, making cleanly retrieving a fly nearly impossible as it was quickly fowled in the weeds. Without encroaching on his personal space I was able to cast into the edge of the hole with my pair of flies. Mirroring his cast, pauses, and retrieving movements

I was soon catching fish. Not rushing to immediately retrieve the fly after it is cast is often important, and here was another blatant example at Henry's Lake. For proactive, impatient fly-anglers who need to be doing "something", pauses and doing nothing to immediately activate the fly can be difficult. Those in the know go s-l-o-w.

Pranking the Fish

Especially in the spring a few silly trout will be more interested in eating my tiny indicator than the flies hanging below it. I have a solution: tie a pupa or nymph on a short tag of line secured to the indicator, and get ready for some angling levity.

When the trout signal they are willing to eat my indicator I prepare by securing a fly near the bubble.

Successfully pranking an indicator-eating fish . . .

Fishing Naked

There are times when stillwater trout are crazy for a fly fished stationary under an indicator but the wind is blowing hard. There are other times when fish have this same presentation preference but I am in the mood for a change of pace, and I want to feel the fish strike the fly

For making longer casts with very long leaders the elevated deck on my drift boat makes an excellent casting platform.

on a tight line. These are situations for some naked fishing, casting and retrieving without an indicator. So, more appropriately, the leader is naked.

As discussed in Chapter 8: Nymphing Leaders for Stillwaters on page 68, this technique involves casting a *floating* fly line to a likely zone, patiently waiting for the flies to sink near the bottom, then creeping the flies back painstakingly slow. Basically, all I am trying to do is keep my line tight in order to detect the strike.

A pivotal puzzle piece in the success of fishing naked is a leader of the correct length. Ideally, the leader length is 25% greater than the water depth. In ten feet of water the leader is 12 1/2 feet long; in twenty feet of water, 25 feet. Obviously, it is imperative I know the depth of the water I am fishing. Toward this end I have previously floated over the area with my electronic depth finder. If I have depleted batteries, and I need to discover the depth, I lock my forceps on my point fly and allow it to descend to the bottom. I then measure the line I have retrieved hand over hand.

Casting very long leaders can be a tricky affair. Proper leader construction is imperative. A breeze will amplify this necessity. A review of Chapter 8 will provide the details.

Some anglers want their nymphs to sink quickly. Lead wire under the fly body, or a tungsten bead at the head accelerate the drop through the water column. The idea is to get the fly down as soon as possible into the "kill zone". However, with an extremely slow retrieve, heavy flies are destined to drag in the silt and vegetation on the bottom, either fouling the hook or crawling ineffectively. It is important to carry patterns of the same size and general design with different amounts of weight. For example, I might have three of the same

Chironomid pupae patterns with differing sink rates. One has a tungsten bead head, the second a standard or plastic bead, while the third has no bead at all.

After I make the cast, I wait only a few seconds before I very slowly retrieve a little line to make sure I have direct contact with the flies, so I can detect even a soft strike since a fish may intercept one of them during the descent. Also, as soon as the flies splash down I begin a countdown. I want to eventually get a sense of the time it takes the flies to reach bottom. It isn't always necessary for the flies to reach bottom before the retrieve begins, so I experiment with when to begin moving the flies in my direction. The slow movements of my retrieve are interspersed with pauses. The exact timing of the pauses and their duration vary, as I experiment. Once I hook a few fish I have a feel of the descent time and exact retrieve the fish prefer.

Just like dangle nymphing I don't want to get caught with my fingers on the fly line, pinching it against the cork grip when a hard strike comes, so I slowly feather the reel spool to retrieve the line. If a violent grab comes it is only the resistance of the reel's precisely-set drag which pulls against the fish. One other advantage of "feathering" the line onto the reel is that there are no coils of line to step on or tangle during the battle.

Go Fully Armed

Successful stillwater nymph fishing is a gear-intensive endeavor. With a broad range of depths and multiple methods to employ, I want to have four different fly lines with me. This means four rods already strung, with flies tied in place and ready to cast. To eliminate the inertia of

I waste little fishing time changing leaders and flies when I carry an arsenal of rods for fishing stillwaters. All are strung and ready before the trip.

assembling rods, stringing lines, and tying on flies when I get to the lake I carry my rods full length and strung in my SUV. I pull them from my vehicle ready to fish.

Because fish in stillwaters have a better chance to inspect a fly before eating it there are times that a more exacting pattern must be selected to fool the fish. Sometimes changing a color shade can make the difference. Fly size, too, can be critical, so I carry my favorite flies in a range from extra small through large. My lake and pond fly boxes fill a small athletic duffel bag.

Steal Lunch for Fly Choice

If I don't have any information or clues about what's happening on a lake I have my favorite flies to begin the day's fishing. For solely fishing nymphs I tie on a size-12 Bead Head Prince paired with a size-12 Skinny Minnie. I can fish these two with any of the techniques and on any of the fly lines I have rigged. I can troll, cast-and-retrieve, or suspend them under an indicator. If I should observe insects over, on, or in the water I may change flies if I am getting no fishing action. Should someone catching fish tell me or hint at what fly is working for them, I may be prompted to switch flies.

An albino rainbow trout ate my Son of Laser Beam Chironomid pupa on a snowy March day.

As I bring my first fish of the day to hand I usually reach for the stomach pump. I have to assume that it may be a long time, or never, before I catch a second fish, so I steal its lunch. In examining the stomach contents I look for a creature that predominates the mix. The best thing I can find in the sample is a broad variety of dining fare, an indication that the fish is not being picky. However, if there is a preferred food item I will select from several thousand flies traveling with me to find the one that best matches it. What I discover may also cause me to switch techniques and fly lines. For instance, I may switch from using a sinking fly line and one of my Frankentroll methods to casting a floating line, suspending Chironomid pupae under an indicator.

Go prepared. Be observant and thoughtful. Make the necessary adjustments to solve the puzzle.

TWELVE

Understanding Steelhead and Planning to Succeed

Steelhead are arguably the world's most exciting freshwater fish. Hard fighting, jumping, unpredictable, challenging, beautiful, heart-stopping, and always memorable, these fish and the experience of catching them can be addictive. I know some fly-anglers who dedicate themselves to pursuing steelhead to the exclusion of all other species, including trout, salmon, bass, and char. It's "all in" on steelhead.

Here's how addiction works. B.F. Skinner, renowned mid-twentieth century psychologist and behaviorist did some very famous experiments with rats in which the rodent was rewarded with a food pellet when it depressed a bar in its cage. Skinner demonstrated that that the bar-hitting behavior could be prompted and reinforced if the rat was rewarded on a *random* basis. If every time Mr. Twinkles hit the bar a pellet appeared, it would depress it only when it wanted food. But, the rat could be conditioned to hit the bar all day if it had no idea when it would be rewarded with a pellet. That is, the reward was randomly occasional, unpredictable.

Steelhead anglers can be conditioned by the fish just like B. F. Skinner trained his rats.

Photo courtesy of WPClipart public domain collection.

Gambling works the same way. For those who love slot machines, the behavior of putting in money and pulling the machine's lever is reinforced to the point of becoming a habit or addiction by randomly winning the occasional jackpot. Sadly, the winnings rarely exceed the total amount of moneys the player is conditioned/ trained to insert into the machine.

For those with a steelhead addiction the same process is at play. After casting hundreds, maybe thousands of times, an angler is rewarded with a big fish on the end of his line. He might catch a fish on his next cast, or on cast #583, or cast #6,122. There is no predicting when the next strike will come. For those with the suited personality, if they stick with it long enough to get the occasional random reward, they can get hooked. Kind of ironic . . . hooked.

Anadromous Rainbow . . . and a Salmon, too

A steelhead is a sea-going rainbow trout, and in recent years also classified as a salmon. The steelhead life cycle and that of the salmon are similar. Both are anadromous: born in freshwater, eventually migrating to saltwater, and return to freshwater to spawn. The major difference between the steelhead and the five Pacific salmon — and it's a huge difference — is that all the original five die after spawning, no ifs, ands, or buts. On the other hand, steelhead are not programmed to die post spawn. They may expire due to injury or exhaustion, but a small, but significant, percentage will return the following year to spawn again. A very special British Columbia hen steelhead was determined through scale analysis to have returned to her home stream six times before being caught and killed by a fisherman.

Not all steelhead returning on their spawning runs are monsters, but often the smaller ones are the scrappiest and most acrobatic of their kind.

Here in the Pacific Northwest most spend two years growing up in freshwater before migrating to the ocean where they can spend one to four years, then return to their home river or stream to spawn. Most in Washington and Oregon will be gone for two years, and return weighing 6 – 10 pounds. This is a generalized range. I have caught steelhead that were 13 inches long, and the fly-caught world record exceeds 30 pounds.

Steelhead Challenge Set

If you are a natural puzzle solver you will love steelhead nymphing. These fabulous fish constantly test any angler's resourcefulness, skills, persistence, and patience. So, to begin, let's survey the playing field and the challenges to be embraced and met.

None for Me, Thanks

Steelhead have evolved whereby they store a tremendous energy reserve in the form of fat tissue while in the ocean. They are constantly dining at the all-you-can-eat buffet. This is similar to what a bear does in northern climes in preparation for hibernating. Fat is stored so that the bear can survive the winter without having to forage for scarce food. As a large organism compared to most resident river trout, there is a chance a steelhead could not find adequate food to survive its spawning journey. To compensate, it has packed its caloric needs into its body. A steelhead can comfortably survive and successfully spawn without eating for seven or eight months. It may occasionally dine to supplement its caloric needs, but appetite seems to be minimal in most.

Challenge #1: The fly-angler is trying to catch a fish that does not need to eat in freshwater before spawning, or which feeds sparsely.

Mark Severson. Fish on!

Is it Time Yet?

Steelhead runs are often not large. Some good streams will have a few fish, some a few hundred, some a few thousand. In bumper crop years there are some large spawning rivers that might hold 10,000 steelhead, or more. Not all fish enter their home streams at the same time. Some summer-run steelhead may return home in May, while others may arrive there in October. Also, if a river is a hundred miles long, or more, there may be an average of only 20, 30, or 40 fish per mile. Compared to resident trout numbers, steelhead per mile aren't many.

Timing the run is important. Some rivers get at least a few steelhead trickling in year-round. Some have one seasonal run of fish. In Oregon, for instance, we have some rivers that have only a winter run of steelhead. This is not a totally accurate depiction of the exact run timing in a winter stream. Some rivers I will begin fishing steelhead in December, while others are not worth my time until February. A few summer-run rivers have fishable numbers of steelhead in May, while July or August mark the beginning of reasonable numbers to fish for in other rivers. A steelhead fly-fisher must know the timing of the runs in any given river before planning a trip for a reasonable chance of success. This presents us with . . .

Challenge #2: There may be few steelhead in the fishing zone. Sometimes there are none. Run timing is critical for any given river.

Don' Forget Your Rain Jacket...and Umbrella?

River levels and water clarity can change wildly, especially in the winter/early spring seasons here in the Pacific Northwest. Unseasonal rains or drought can affect summer and fall river conditions.

Even in the summer, thunder showers can roll through. Staying dry helps maintain focus and enthusiasm, important elements since steelhead strike opportunities are few in a typical fishing day.

River conditions fluctuate. Water levels range from flood stage in the winter to low, clear, and too warm in the summertime. At the extremes, and points near them, steelhead can be taken totally out of the biting mood, or cannot be approached to get into a fishable position to tempt the fish to bite. I postpone a good number of winter steelhead guide trips because the water conditions are too high or too low. In the heat of summer, steelhead may retreat into slow, deep unfishable pools, where they can become lethargic in warm water.

Challenge #3: The river and weather conditions can adversely affect the fish and the fishing.

Do You Mind if I Cast Over Your Line?

Every angler wants to catch big fish. Steelhead create a lot of excitement when the word gets out the fish are in the river, and fishing reports entice the hordes to flock there to try their luck. This can be an unpleasant social interaction as fishermen jockey for position with each other. Steelhead tend to linger in very specific water types. These prime, and often small, sections of fishing real estate often draw more anglers than the space can accommodate. Sometimes civility falls by the wayside. So, some of us will avoid steelhead fishing crowds at all cost. Crowding can be a huge challenge to deal with on some steelhead rivers.

When these fish are small in number, and they prefer very specific water types, of which there is not an abundance, all interested and knowledgeable steelhead fishermen end up in the same small places at the same time. As within any group, some have no respect for another man or woman's personal space. They can be rude, disrespectful. I encounter this often on steelhead rivers. Every angler has many stories about disrespectful, boorish behavior as other anglers encroach on them, often casting their lines into the same small piece of water in an attempt to catch the steelhead there. And, every steelhead angler has stories, either as participant or observer, where the encroacher is confronted, and then tries to loudly and abrasively justify his right to trespass. My favorite hackneyed retort by the rude angler is: "You don't own the river!" To which I might reply: "And you don't possess a hint of reasonable courtesy."

The problem has arisen and been enabled by the fact that over decades of conditioning, steelhead fishermen have come to accept shoulder-to-shoulder fishing as the accepted norm. I would be remiss if I did not point to the fact that I have not ever seen this to be true for fly-anglers. Never.

My Number 1 steelheading challenge — successfully competing with numerous other anglers.

When it comes to successfully meeting the challenge of crowding — at this juncture in my long steelheading career — I must dedicate more time to this aspect of my strategic fish-catching game plan than all other facets combined. My Sudoku puzzles are rated on a scale from Easy to Expert. Overcoming the crowding issue demands successfully solving an Expert-level puzzle. Getting to the river before daybreak is not the solution, as many anglers might think.

Welcome to the party!

Early summer of 2014, two of my former OSU students, who are also my occasional fishing companions, launched a drift boat before sunrise on the South Santiam River in pursuit of steelhead. They were the tenth(!) boat to launch that morning. And, there were at least two dozen boats that launched after them, according to their end-of-the-day calculations. So this day there were more than 30 drift boats . . . on a three-mile section of river! There was no escape from the hordes in this situation. As for their catching success, Jason and Greg, two very experienced and skilled fly-anglers, did

not touch a single steelhead for their efforts. So, you may think it good to launch early and push down the river ahead of the crowd, but it doesn't work too well when ten other guys have the same idea. And, in only three miles of water you will quickly run out of river. Better have a Plan B.

Challenge #4: A crowded, competitive fishing environment can upset the fish (those which survive the onslaught) and the fishermen. When river conditions are reasonable, this is often the biggest challenge to catching steelhead. In my experience this is the leading reason why many fly-anglers give up steelhead to pursue trout exclusively.

We've Got to Go Back! I Forgot My . . .

People forget or overlook things, myself included. As a guide, where I oversee all activities and provide all the fishing gear, if needed, I try to leave my stowed gear untouched and in its place at the conclusion of our fishing from day to day. All my gear stays in my 4Runner, set up and ready to load into my boat. The only thing that gets unloaded for next-day prep is my cooler, so I may replenish the ice and create tomorrow's lunch.

Alarm fails. Client forgets license. Cameras, spare camera batteries, and failure to charge cell phones for photography purposes are — by far — at the top of the "I forgot to . . ." list. Trailer lights are forever shorting out and wires pull loose. Bathroom emergencies happen. Coffee stops are absolutely necessary for some. There's a weekend fly-fishing club outing on my section of river. Yikes! I try to embrace all these challenges in order stay sane and be a cordial host.

Challenge #5: Expect delays and derailments which will disrupt the day's strategic game plan. Have contingencies and backups.

A waterproof point & shoot camera can add fun to the fishing day.

When my anchor is prone to sliding along the bottom in waters bordering good holding water I may choose to be the "anchor". Yes, this is above and beyond the call of duty for most guides.

Lazy Is As Lazy Does

M. Scott Peck wrote one of my favorite books of all time: *The Road Less Traveled.* As a psychiatrist he encountered many interesting people with an array of mental and emotional problems which he attempted to help his clients resolve. He had stories of great successes, and many cases where the problems of his patients were never fixed, even though the solutions to the maladies were understood, and the direct course to resolution became obvious. Patients that had worked with Peck for years to determine what finally needed to be done *by the patient strictly through their own efforts* for the permanent "fix" they often failed to do because it required work and discipline. What Peck concludes from these prevalent failures is that what we all share as human beings is the inclination toward laziness.

The *consistently* successful steelhead angler has found a way to power past laziness — laziness about planning and preparation — to do what is necessary to implement an effective plan to find and catch steelhead. In my case, especially when I am guiding, my fear of failure overwhelms my tendency toward laziness. I am a pleaser, which is a dangerous attribute for dealing with the uncertainties of steelhead fishing. I need to enable my clients and guests to catch steelhead.

No matter what I might earn for a day's work on a steelhead river, what means much more is that my clients hook fish and have a good time doing so.

Pride, too, is an additional motivator for me. At the end of the day I need a "Yes!" answer to one question: Did I do my very best as a guide today? Three of the things which enable me to answer "Yes!" are thorough planning, maximum preparation, and exceptional physical effort. This last item means I will row my tail off to position my drift boat so my clients will be exactly where they need to be to catch a fish, and rowing upstream against powerful currents to re-run a productive piece of water, if necessary. If needed, I am a human anchor. *Every* day. No laziness allowed.

Challenge #6: Overcome laziness. I will plan and prepare as if today's steelheading outing is my last.

Creating a Strategic Game Plan

When it comes to athletics, football is my game. I coached secondary school football for seven years in a prior life, and I have taught flag football at Oregon State. Early in my teaching career I was fortunate to be on the coaching staff of an undefeated high school team which won a state football championship. As you might guess, planning and preparation were imperative to winning it all.

There is much to consider in building a successful steelhead fishing day, especially in a competitive fishing environment. Success is much, much more than a box of killer flies and mad fishing skills.

Every fishing day is different: weather, water, river traffic, skills and experience of my companions or guests, section of river to be fished, river hazards, contingencies for the unexpected that may affect fishing success, comfort, enjoyment, and safety. I want to anticipate the adjustments that might be needed, and assess what my reasonable options are, all the while looking to gain a competitive advantage for my clients and guests.

Though I have included my game plan creation here in a steelhead chapter, the suggestions presented below are certainly applicable to trout fishing in rivers, too. Most of the same challenges are in play, with the exception of run timings, appetites of the fish, and numbers of fish.

Game Plan Element #1

Who am I fishing with today? Clients? Are they newbies or experienced? Friends and family? Or, do I get to fish alone today, just me and my camera?

For clients and guests I will be fishing from my boat, with a few exceptions. With my boat I can cover a lot more distance and water. My anglers will not have to wade, which is important as a time-saver and a safety issue. Also, when a fish is hooked there is a higher probability of the steelhead being landed since I can chase it, staying right on top of the fish if necessary. I can coach my guest through every nuance of successfully playing and landing the fish.

Always looking for a steelheading edge sometimes entails launching my boat where others can't or won't.

If I am fishing alone I may want to stay on foot. I may choose, then, to do hit-and-run surgical strikes on those pieces of water miles below the nearest boat launch long before boaters will be able to reasonably float and fish the distance necessary to reach me. Or, I may fish the upper section of a river where boats cannot safely go. As for competing with other on-foot anglers, I may venture up the trail much farther than them, or bushwhack into areas where others cannot or will not go.

Be willing to pay the price for getting to the steelhead where others can't or won't go.

Game Plan Element #2

River choice is, of course, of paramount importance. Those who aspire to maximize their catch must dedicate the time necessary to create a comprehensive experiential catalog of steelhead rivers. An angler limiting himself to knowing well only one or two rivers has limited options, especially since steelhead runs in any river are of limited duration. And, when in-season river conditions are not suitable on river choices 1 and 2, river options 3, 4, and 5 must be known.

Tom Clements demonstrates good fighting form — high rod tip and no hands or fingers on the line or fly reel.

On Oregon's north coast I have seven winter steelhead rivers all within 45 minutes of each other. So, in light of the considerations for my guests, or whether I will be fishing by myself, I have river choices. In the mid Willamette Valley of Oregon I have multiple choices for summer steelhead.

Every river has its own steelhead run timing. Rivers A and B are at their primes in December and January. Rivers C and D fish best February and March. River E produces late December through mid April.

Some steelhead rivers have temperamental flows, easily going to unfishable with a heavy rain or lack of rain. Others are dam-controlled, and the flows are more consistent and dependable.

Some rivers are very accessible throughout their entire length, with few safe havens to escape other anglers. If I am on foot, I much prefer a river where access is not so easy, counting on the anglers to be lazy or unwilling to get to those productive locations which require effort and time.

River Research Resources

Steelhead fishing contacts: Most of us have friends "in the know", or have other fishing friends that may know about quality steelhead rivers. It is always best to treat valuable fishing information as privileged, not to be shared with thousands of others on the fishing forum at SecretSteelheadInformation.com.

Local fly shop: This can *possibly* be a good data-mining location. Dropping by a shop in person — which means you have the opportunity to contribute some financial support to the business — you may be able to glean some valuable fishing information about where to catch a steelhead. Flies and tippet don't spoil. Though I have a million flies and miles of tippet, I always find more to buy at a helpful fly-fishing establishment. I can guarantee you a phone call to a shop where they do not know you as a loyal customer will get you very little valuable, non-generic information.

State Department of Fish & Wildlife: Perusing their website, look for steelhead rivers that are referenced. Rivers mentioned which you've never thought of or heard about are worth investigating. The online annual fishing regulations handbook will reference some steelhead streams that were not on your radar. Once discovered, do some research. Also, if you are interested in rivers with abundant numbers of hatchery steelhead for your dining pleasure, discover which rivers have hatcheries on them. Also, hatchery steelhead returns to date may be available online or with a phone call, giving a good indication of the availability of fish in the river.

Books, magazines, TV, and DVDs: These can be good informational sources to discover where, when, how, and with what. I read many magazine articles and books looking for something new and useful, sometimes even re-reading portions of my own book, *Steelhead Fly Angling* (Frank Amato Publications, 2012). Even though there is a universe of information available, there is no substitute for personal experience and thoughtful efforts on the water.

Professional fishing guides: Guides must go where the fish are. Their websites are opportunities to discover the rivers they fish, and the time of year that they guide them. You can "shortcut the system" by booking the guide for a fishing trip to learn the river.

Internet chat and fishing reports: The Chatosphere can afford some informational tidbits. There are popular fishing forums out there easily discovered with an Internet search. Rivers that are fishing well, including rivers you may never have heard of and will want to research, will be discussed at such sites.

For a new river I will create a file folder in which to collect information I am going to gather. Maps detailing parks, bridges, boat launches, and campgrounds; supply stores, shuttle service, accommodations; and fishing reports that mention specific flies, specific sections of river to consider, and access points.

Game Plan Element #3

I have my chosen stream, but which portion of the river will I fish tomorrow?

Fish concentration: At this time in the fishing season, where in the river are the most fish to be found? Early in the season the fish tend to be most numerous in the lower and mid-river portions. Late in the season the biggest numbers can be in the upper river. Mid season they are spread throughout.

At any given time certain sections of river are fishing better than adjacent portions. For whatever reason a wave of fish has come up the river as a unit and is concentrated in the eight miles of river between Bridge A and County Park Z, and I did well here today. Logic dictates I fish the same section tomorrow. Or, conversely, the section of river I fished today produced few fish, so I will fish a different section tomorrow.

River conditions: Last night it rained hard. Certain tributaries will bring muddy water to raise and influence the water clarity. Or, the glacially-fed White River on the Deschutes is melting hard and is pumping dirty water into the Deschutes, blowing out the river from that point to the mouth for several days or more. Or, the river is low due to drought, so fishing the river below several tributaries which introduce more and cooler water into the river makes good sense.

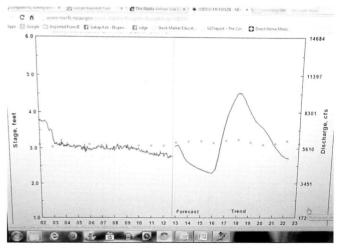

Part of good steelhead trip planning is knowing the current and projected river conditions.

Online hydrograph data is indispensable: Besides showing the river level, a current hydrograph reading shows the trend of the river level. And, some sites project near term water flows taking into consideration the weather forecast for the next week or ten days. If planning a trip in the next

Those who boat Western steelhead rivers had better know what's around the corner. Greg Schuerger successfully navigates a major rapids on Oregon's Nehalem River. Not for fools or the faint of heart.

few days, and a massive rainstorm is coming in very soon, the river could be blown out by the time I arrive, resulting in wasted travel and fruitless fishing possibilities. Especially in the winter and early spring, my decision to fish lives and dies with hydrographical forecasts.

Access barriers: This can be both good and bad. It works to my favor if I'm boating the river. Most anglers are on foot, without a boat. Private property is a barrier. Access may be available only at parks and bridges.

Dangerous rapids through which I can safely pass can be deterrents to others with less knowledge or boating skills. I personally seek out such sections of rivers to separate myself from the pack.

Some rivers which require serious wading to access the steelhead can be treacherous. Even small rivers can challenge the weak or timid wader as you make your way along them or cross them where necessary. Wading shoe soles with studs and a wading staff may be necessary. The plus to such waters is less competition.

Access roadways can present difficulties, which can work for the adventuresome steelheader. Some stream portions are difficult to get to because it necessitates negotiating a puzzle of logging roads to find the river.

If you do find your way in, can you find your way out? Such roads can be in serious disrepair. Large puddles, deep mud, fallen trees, and steep, bouldered grades make passage dangerous. Four-wheel drive has saved me many times. To overcome such sketchy accesses makes any steelhead caught in solitude that much sweeter.

Game Plan Element #4

Though I could have included this as part of the Step 3 planning process, the interplay of other anglers, both boaters and bank fishermen, is so important I have given it a separate section by itself for emphasis.

With more than three decades of steelhead fly-fishing experience, I know my single biggest obstacle to the success of my fishing, or that of my guided clients, will be other anglers. And, not just from boating fishermen, but from bank anglers, too, in certain areas. For me, thinking through many "what if" scenarios involving other fishermen receives most of my planning time for tomorrow's fishing.

If I do find another boat ahead of me near or in the water I want to target I must assess the effectiveness of their fishing knowledge and skills, or whether he is

When the masses arrive there had better be a Plan B, Plan C, Plan D ...

fishing with a good guide. This will drive my decision to push ahead or lay back. First, I want to see what angling method is being used. A boat fishing diving plugs may very well bypass faster riffles and runs, while I choose to fish these. Secondly, I want to pay attention to the specific water being fished. If my experience tells me the anglers are fishing water where there is virtually no chance of finding a resting steelhead I will not hesitate to fish the productive water that has been overlooked. Another simple gauge of an angler's experience and skill is the ability to smoothly and accurately cast. Poor casters are rarely a threat to the steelhead I want to catch.

Two of the most crucial decisions I make while fishing is how long I linger in any one fishing spot and where and when to go when we encounter other anglers. If I cannot find enough available fishing water because of the persistent presence of boating and bank anglers — even on a nine-mile section of river — part of my game plan can involve an early delivery of my vehicle to the take-out point by my shuttle driver. I then have the option to pull out early, and launch a second time that day on a different section of river. I have had occasions where I have left a river early and travelled to *another* river to fish the second half of the day in order to beat the crowds.

It is imperative that I have secondary fishing locations on any given river that I may fall back on when the river is busy. Though they are not my first choices of water to be fished, they can produce the occasional steelhead and keep my anglers satisfied with their day on the water. Interestingly, some of the locations initially relegated to second class have become first-tier locations once I fished them more frequently and came

to understand where the fish hold and how to best approach them.

I have a location on the Rogue River I refer to as Magic Rock. For years it was one of my secondary spots which I bypassed as often as I fished it. Over the years, as I experimented with my boat position, and carefully mapped specific lines of drift at Magic Rock, it began to produce on a *very* consistent basis. In fact, I have come to expect my clients or I will hook a steelhead here every time I anchor here. If we don't hook a fish I assume someone has fished it before we did. In the late summer of 2014 client Karl "Bigfish" Brantley hooked four steelhead on nymphs in about 45 minutes at Magic Rock. Coincidently, to speak to the effectiveness of nymph fishing for steelhead, prior to fishing nymphs in this spot, Karl very effectively covered all the Magic Rock water with proven wet flies on a sink-tip fly line. I know that every fish he later hooked saw his wet fly first, and had the wet fly-fished to them as well as it can be presented. For many, many such similar demonstrations the steelhead's preference for nymphs over wet flies, I never hesitate to fish behind a wet-fly fisherman. Even if they catch a fish in the water I will fish after them. The only fly-angler who can strike fear in my heart is another effective nymph fisher. "Effective" is the operative word here. Many aspire to fish nymphs; most are not effective.

Game Plan Element #5

One of the key strategies for maximizing steelhead *catch* is maximizing fishing *time*. It's a numbers game: the more good casts that are made into likely steelhead holding water, the greater the chance of hooking a fish. Ultimately, this where all of my preparation is aimed.

I have to shake my head a little as I watch anglers, including those being guided, spend the first twenty minutes of their fishing day stringing rods, tying on leaders, finding the right fly, and wasting precious fishing time. Once fishing commences, with only one rod, leader reconstruction and fly replacement take time away from fishing. Tangled lines can demand more chunks of time.

To address these issues, I have multiple rods strung up and ready to fish the night before. Actually, I like my rods set-up before we depart the river at the fishing day's conclusions. They ride in my 4Runner strung and flies tied in place. I am carrying extra rods, too, strung and loaded as all the others. When an untimely break-off happens, or a massive tangle occurs, I hand my guests another rod while I deal with the repairs. Even if anglers are fishing their own rods, I will hand them one of mine. If a guest has two rods of their own I encourage

Put an indicator, split shot, and multiple flies on the same leader and let the casting fun begin. Water-load the cast and use grandiose — not staccato — rod tip movements to minimize tangling.

them to do as I do, to have them set-up and ready to cast the night before.

As for flies, I carry many, and I monitor my supply to make sure that I have plenty of my most productive nymphs and egg patterns. My clients are provided with a list of flies they will need, but I must make sure they have access to what they need as they run low.

The only preparation of items that must be replenished each day is lunches. My boating and fishing gear are ready to go for Day 2 by the time we leave the river at the conclusion of Day 1. Even when I my boat is in the garage at home waiting for the next trip, the assembled rods are waiting in the boat. All I need do is place the rods in my rig, hook-up the boat trailer, throw the cooler in the boat, and I am down the road ready to fish.

Many effective steelhead nymphs are trout nymphs tied on relatively small hooks. Even after many warnings from his guide one of my guests insisted on grabbing the reel handle to prevent a steelhead from running away.

Game Plan Element #6

There are some miscellaneous considerations that influence my planning. These include planning for the unexpected or unanticipated.

Equipment failure: Broken rods, reels that don't work, waders that spring a leak, boat problems, a broken oar, raft or pontoon boat puncture, these are a few of the more common items to go haywire. Every wader and every boater has a story. In decades of fishing I have many anecdotes about all of the mentioned items, some of them harrowing.

Oars, as you would guess, are essential to controlling a drift boat's path down the river. This leads me to the single most concerning unexpected equipment failure I ever confront. When an oar breaks, or comes out of the oarlock, control is lost. So, when one or the other of these situations occurs — always in treacherous whitewater — safety is a crucial issue. Luckily, in more than thirty years of running whitewater rivers I have never sunk a boat or had a guest injured in a boating accident.

There are some key elements to a safe recovery in a boating mishap. The first is that I have to be calm and calmly authoritative. My demeanor will set the tone with my guests, who may lean toward panic, so I do a bit of mental prep in this regard. Life jackets must be quickly secured, if they are not already being worn. I continue to talk to my clients, doing my best to reassure them and keep them calm. I prepare them for the inevitability of an impact and that they may need to shift their weight on my command.

Secondly, I must be able to instantly assess the best safe solution to regaining control of the boat. If needed, a third oar is always at hand, ready to be put in place. I can usually buy a little time and space with the one oar still in the water, making sure, as best I can, we do not hit an obstruction broadside, whereby the boat may capsize. Instead, if a collision is to occur, I want it to be head on. I have the experience and capability to run a piece of whitewater backwards, if I must. I practice this. It's like backing a car down a winding road. It can be done.

Lastly, if we get lodged on a boulder or rock outcropping it is most often a matter of weight distribution for getting free. If both passengers are in the front of the stuck boat, I may ask the more nimble of the two to relocate to the rear seat behind me. I caution the moving passenger that the boat may shift as they reposition, and what they must do to maintain their balance and safety. If the weight redistribution is not a solution by itself I will direct the passengers to rock the boat with me, or, in some cases, jump up and down while I push

Note the wrecked boat in the lower left quadrant of the photo as I negotiate White Horse rapids on the Deschutes River.

and pull on the oars to free the boat. Continuing with my calm demeanor, I warn them that we will most likely come off the obstruction backwards, and that will be okay. My prime directive, again, will be to prevent hitting another rock broadside.

Once we are free of our whitewater "thrill", I continue to cultivate an attitude of calm as we continue our fishing day. I don't minimize the danger, as such, but point to a plan which I created and they helped me implement to ensure our safety. These incidents always make for inevitable and lively conversation in the future. Overlooking this part of a strategic fishing game plan when a boat or raft is involved is a serious matter.

Safety and first aid: Maybe you are healthy and safety conscious, but your fishing companions may not be. My dad had a heart condition. When we dropped into a river canyon or ascended a mountain trail this was a concern. My worst leg/ankle/toe injuries have occurred wading in rivers.

Protective glasses are a safety necessity for the caster, his companions, and the guide. Another brilliant case for barbless hooks.

Cell phone communication? Many rivers have no cell phone reception. How will you get help? A first-aid kit can be assembled and placed in a zip-lock bag, containing a few bandages, antibacterial wipes, an antibacterial/pain-relieving cream or ointment, and ibuprofen tablets.

Vehicle problems. I have had the start of an early morning road trip delayed as I waited an hour or more for a gas station to open. What about that soft tire I forgot to check? As

Nymph fishing success! Katie Zajicek on her first steelhead fly-fishing trip.

I prepare to leave, the tire is flat.

Routine maintenance cannot be ignored. My friend Jeff got two (!) flat tires simultaneously on a nasty gravel road. No one I know carries two spares. Fortunately I happened along that day returning from a guided trip, and gave him a ride to the nearest town more than ten miles away.

On several occasions I have hit a deer, damaging my vehicle. It's amazing how effective honking as I anticipate the collision will move the deer out of my headlights. **Items often forgotten.** Fishing license. Credit card/cash. Driver's license. Sunglasses/eye protection. Sunscreen. Wading shoes. Fishing vest. Rain jacket. Gloves. Lunch. Backpack. Cell phone. Phone number for shuttle. Camera. Camera batteries. Maps & directions.

Like a pilot does before takeoff, make a checklist. Buy more time to hook more steelhead.

So . . .

In light of the challenges I have just laid out, catching a steelhead on a fly demands serious planning. It's much more than going to a likely river when the fish are present, trusting you will find a piece of water where you can fish without intrusion, and covering likely areas with your favorite nymphs or egg patterns. It's impossible, I think, to over-plan. Like preparing for the big game, plan to maximize your fish-catching opportunities, and do it safely. Resist being lazy. As I tell my students: Make your momma proud. Daddy, too.

All-Star Steelhead Nymphs and Egg Flies

As the chapter title indicates I am including a few of my favorite egg patterns for steelhead, for a couple of reasons. First, egg flies are fished using the nymph fishing method. For summer and fall fishing, when I use an egg, it is always paired with a nymph. Secondly, when I nymph for steelhead in the winter and early spring my clients and I use egg patterns and their derivatives exclusively. It's a stretch, but if you are a stickler, think of an actual fish egg as the nymphal stage of a young steelhead or salmon.

My all-star steelhead nymphs are a mix of realistic, impressionistic, and Frankenstein. Some look very much like the insect it is meant to imitate, like Kaufmann's Stonefly Nymph. Others are general representations of something intriguingly yummy, like the Bead Head Prince. Then, there are flies such as my Princely Stoneflies in which I have stolen body parts from other patterns and added a touch of psychedelic to create Frankenflies.

I am always on the lookout for new steelhead nymphs. When I go into a fly shop I gravitate to the nymphs, looking specifically for flies that have "the look" for steelhead. I buy two or three of those that intrigue me to experiment with. Occasionally, I find one that actually catches fish. Or, I will discover a nymph that has an interesting element about it which I may incorporate into a new fly I create. Though I know I will never find it, I am always searching for the Holy Grail steelhead nymph, one which no steelhead can resist. It adds to the fun of trying to seduce these picky wonderful fish.

Metallic tail, goose biot wings, Midnight Fire chenille, and hot pink rubber legs. My **Princely Stone** (next page top left), and imaginative variations of it, catch steelhead. It isn't a close match to a real stonefly nymph but there is something intriguing about this gaudy Frankenfly that steelhead like. Like a lot. Sizes 6 & 8.

One of two flies that made all the All-Star teams, the **Flashback Hare's Ear** is an excellent choice when the steelhead prefer a fly that looks more natural and buggy. In appropriate sizes this fly is a passable imitation of mayflies, caddisflies, and stoneflies. And steelhead will take them even in tiny sizes sometimes. I once caught a 6-pound steelhead fishing a size-20 Hare's Ear for trout on the Deschutes River. Sizes 10 – 14.

Shiny metal can get a steelhead's attention. Flashy spinners and spoons have caught countless steelhead for generations. The **Copper John** is tied in a variety of fun colors. I like copper, red, green, chartreuse, and blue. Sizes 10 – 14.

The **Kaufmann's Bead Head Rubber Leg Stonefly** nymph has lived in steelhead fly boxes for many years. Its realistic buggy appearance will readily fool a steelhead looking for an oversize snack. It's also the heaviest fly I carry. When likely holding water is deep and fast this fly drops quickly into The Zone. Sizes 6 – 10.

Here it is for the third time, the ubiquitous **Prince Nymph**. This is the fly that convinced me forever that steelhead will eat small flies intended to catch trout. A size-14 standard Prince Nymph was my staple "little" fly for summer steelhead for many years. Sizes 10 – 14.

The Scorpion has everything a steelhead wants in a fly design — dark body with pearlescent highlights, variegated rubber legs, sexy orange bead head, white goose biots, and a soft hackle to further convey life. This fly is definitely a steelhead All-Star.

Another good trout fly, the **Rubber Leg Fox Squirrel Nymph** is a steelhead enticer, especially in those streams with larger caddisfly species. When the *Dicosmoecus* caddisflies, October Caddis, begin hatching in late September, this pattern is a convincing imitation of the pupa. Sizes 8 – 12.

Besides being a good attractor pattern, the orange color theme of the **Jumbo John** finds this fly with enhanced effectiveness at fall salmon spawning time. It has the appearance of an egg-sucking alien insect. Works for me. Size 6.

My **Gorman Golden Stonefly**, rubber-leg version, has the right shade of golden brown Angora dubbing fur. Most golden stone patterns have a dubbing that is too gold, or too yellow. Larger species have a three-year life cycle and are available to fish year-round. Sizes 6 & 8.

I can't have too many stonefly patterns in my steelhead nymph box. The **Mega Prince's** peacock body and lively rubber legs will sometimes be the fly *du jour*. Sizes 6 – 10.

There are many egg-fly designs. I've tried them all. When my clients *need* to catch steelhead during the winter and fall seasons, my **Bead Head Egg** is a workhorse. Tied in shades of pink and orange with an egg yarn veil, this fly is fished with confidence, knowing that if a steelhead is interested in eating a salmon egg it will take this one. Sizes 6 – 10.

If the water is quick and deep I want an egg that will drop to the bottom quickly, my **Dumbbell Sparkle Egg** is the choice. I often pair it with a lightly weighted Bead Head Egg where the Dumbbell Egg acts a weight to put both flies near the bottom. Shades of pink and orange sparkle chenille. Sizes 6 – 10

My **Hot Bead Assassin** has been the final evolutionary point of flies I developed and fished for steelhead for years. Especially when the river has a bit of color due to recent rain, I pair this fly with one of my egg flies. Though it has a wet-fly design I most often fish it dead-drift. If tied at the point position on the leader I get the added swing presentation of the wet fly and the possibility of a hard grab when the line comes tight. Two techniques on one cast. Size 6.

In heavily fished steelhead waters where the fish have seen a lot of flies day after day, sometimes a little attention-grabbing glitz is the trigger. Enter the **Bling Egg**. Inspired by a fly tied by Jay Nicholas I dubbed the "SquEgg", the Bling has accounted for many steelhead. In fact it is so good it had to be included on my All-Star team.

FOURTEEN

Precise Details for Effective Steelhead Nymphing

Keegan Warrington lifts high after the scoop for Jason Mariner.

The fish are few, but the rewards are big. Fooling a steelhead into taking a nymph is a rush, especially when the angler stops to consider the numerous challenges that have been successfully met. The timing, the river, the chosen piece of water, the gear, the flies, the technique, and the presence of a willing fish must all be right. There is a very good reason these spectacular creatures are referred to as a fish of a thousand casts. Every steelhead is earned and special.

There are many details that go into the effective nymph fishing. More than the reader could begin to know. The killer rod, reel, line, leader, flies, precision casting, and perfect mending mechanics aren't always enough to put a steelhead on the end of the line. There are circumstances, unexpected problems, other anglers, and mysterious intangibles at play which can stand in

the way of fishing success. If I ignore or forget them, I am limiting the fish-catching possibilities for me and my clients. Because steelhead are temperamental, have little or no appetite, and they are few in number, the importance of precision mending, detecting strikes which can be subtle, and executing the correct hook-set are all magnified. There are precious few chances in a typical steelheading day.

Hard Reality — Deal with It!

There are three "realities": 1) Reality as we think it is, that is, as we perceive it. 2) Reality as we *hope* it to be. 3) Reality as it truly is. Better known as "harsh reality". We are going to deal with Number 3.

Here are some steelheading facts you, dear reader, will have to come to terms with:

1. Steelhead do not have to eat during their spawning run. The best flies fished with skilled nymphing precision may fail to entice a steelhead.

2. Compared to the numbers of trout in a quality steelhead river, steelhead are not very numerous when measured in fish per mile.

3. Other steelhead anglers want to catch *your* fish. Too many will rudely interact with our attempts. This can seriously derail the enjoyment of the fishing day.

4. Murphy's Law is always at play: delays, ill-equipped or "needy" fishing companions, equipment failure, tangles, break-offs, wading mishaps, forgotten items, dead cameras, and drowned cell phones. These are just a few elements in Murphy's game.

5. One's state of mind, attitude, patience, and resiliency can all influence the fish-catching outcome, and often do. Often. Believe it!

6. As a professional fishing guide I have to deal with an additional element of reality — guests who will not, or cannot, follow my directions.

After a long fight, a tired buck steelhead comes to hand for Mark Kaczmarek.

The Steelheading Mindset

I have encountered many fly-anglers who are not psychologically suited to fishing for steelhead. These anglers want results in short order, but it often doesn't work to their expectations. Most of us come from a trout fishing background. Trout eat on a regular basis, but steelhead do not once they have returned to freshwater on their spawning journeys. Most steelhead, therefore, have to be cajoled, wooed, enticed. A steelhead nympher has to be a skilled salesperson who enjoys the challenge, with the knowledge that rejection is part of the process. I find it helpful to *embrace* the challenges that are sure to come. Also, I find when I take a little time to appreciate the beautiful settings in which steelhead are found, and enjoy the clients and guests who share the river with me for the day, I am not overwhelmed with impatience as I wait for the strike to come. Casting and mending have a pleasant rhythm to them, and offer their own satisfaction as I strive to make each one perfect.

Make no mistake — I intensely want to catch steelhead. When I am guiding clients, my intensity is ratcheted up another two notches. Often I am both a guide and a psychologist. As a steelhead guide/psychologist it is my job to keep my guests upbeat, hopeful, attentive, and on high alert for the possibility a fish might intercept their nymph. This is not an easy task working with those personalities focused on catching a steelhead NOW! I do my best, but in order to do so I am my own "patient", quietly counseling myself. I must work at keeping my exterior calm, collected, and upbeat.

Rather than slightly elevating the fish's head creating more current push against a big fish, a low-fighting rod tip keeps the head and body horizontal, more hydrodynamic, enabling better control of the steelhead.

An upbeat positive attitude is extremely important to steelheading success. When I tell my clients this I always sense skepticism. But I have seen this play out so many times over decades of steelhead fishing it is unbelievable. This is one of Unexplainable Rules of the Universe. I see it frequently when an inexperienced angler is paired with an "expert" who has brought the novice as a guest. The rookie, or casual angler, has low expectations of steelhead-catching success but are willing participants in the pursuit. They tend to be good at following my directions. The "expert" figures he will easily outfish his guest, and is often anxious about demonstrating his mad skills, so he presses hard. Too hard. Things go haywire with snags and tangles and little frustrations when the fish are being stubborn.

When the indicator goes down veteran steelheading nympher Joann Severson knows exactly what to do to get the fish to the boat.

And, of course, the less experienced angler will usually outfish the expert. This is borne out most frequently by men fishing with their spouse or girlfriend. The woman has a great upbeat attitude, knowing that the likelihood of catching a steelhead is not great, so they are happy to be on a beautiful river, enjoying the sights, the conversation, and the company. The steelhead seem to respond to this, and jump on the rookie's flies.

Another one of my Rules of the Universe is played out when an angler states he "*needs* to catch a fish", or has promised someone(s) he will bring a steelhead home for dinner. Steelhead do not respond well to these

demands. I'm not superstitious. My university education is science and math. However, I'm at a rational loss to know why steelhead respond to an angler's attitude. All I know for sure is that a cheery, upbeat mindset tremendously increases the odds of steelhead-catching success. The reader ignores this observation at his (or her) own steelheading peril.

Summer vs. Winter

Here in the Pacific Northwest we have two general steelhead seasons: winter and summer. Migrating "summer" steelhead enter freshwater over a very broad range of months, some as early as May, and some as late as October. The spawning timing for the majority is January through March. "Winter" steelhead come in late November through April, and most will spawn in the February through April timeframe.

Though I will fish the same water types summer and winter, the fishes' behavior will differ a bit with the season, as will nymph fly preferences. Wintertime water temperatures ranging from upper 30's to mid 40's take steelhead out of their optimal comfort zone, which is upper 40's to 60 degrees Fahrenheit. With a few exceptions, of course, winter steelhead will not move as far to intercept a fly as summer steelhead in the comfortable water temperatures of late spring through mid fall. In cold flows my fishing pace is slower.

When the water is cold, fish low, slow, and cover likely spots very, very meticulously with little distance between successive drifts of the flies.

For summer steelhead in rivers where the water temp is in the optimal temperature range I will fish a piece of water methodically and thoroughly, then, move on. In the winter I will fish the same piece of water at a slower pace, with more casts, anticipating that I must eventually get a slow drift of my flies very close — perhaps a few inches — to a holding fish in order to interest it. On occasions when I have been able to cast to holding

├─── 3' 30 lb. mono ───┼─────   ├── 1' .012" fluoro + 3' fluoro tippet ──┤

2' - 6' fast sinking shooting head

winter steelhead I can see in front of me, I have come to appreciate actually how near my flies must be to the fish before it will intercept the nymph or egg pattern.

Also, I find it productive for winter fish in particular to present them with an alternative presentation to the standard dead-drift of the flies under an indicator.

Steelhead FrankenNymphing — The Hybrid Line System

Back in the early 1980s I had a steelhead fly-fishing problem. Throughout my fishing day I cover a lot of water. In doing so I finish a broad spectrum of combinations of water speed and depth. For instance, at the top of the run I can be fishing likely water that is slow moving and 4 feet deep. Then, as I drop into the heart of the run, I am searching in water that is 7 feet deep and quick paced. To get the perfect drift of the fly in both combinations, adjustments to the line or leader or fly must be made. If not, my fly can drift perfectly through one combination, but above the fish or dragging the bottom in the other situation.

One solution would be for me to carry a handful of strong fly rods with different syncing lines on them. Then, like a golfer selecting a club from his bag, I would pick the appropriate rod with the correct line on it for the given combination of current speed in depth that I am currently fishing. Though this is a possible answer,

Sometimes the timing of the photo is embarrassingly perfect!

it's not a very practical one if I am fishing on foot, which I often do when fishing steelhead by myself.

Another possible change I could affect is to tie weighted and un-weighted versions of all the flies I would use. There are two downside effects of weighted flies — they do not swim and drift as naturally in the current as un-weighted flies, and weighted flies are more prone to getting snagged on the river bottom.

Adding or removing split shot from the leader can fine-tune the drift of the flies, matching the amount of weight to the current speed and depth. Unfortunately, the addition of weight to the leader is not legal in fly-fishing-only waters, like Oregon's North Umpqua and upper Rogue rivers.

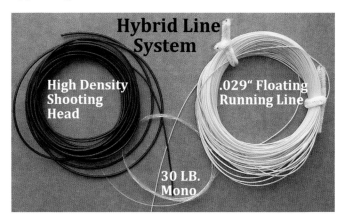

I wanted one line system to accommodate my needs — a quick effective adjustable set-up to create an effective drift of the flies, again, matched to the current velocity and depth. So, from this need I created what I came to call my Hybrid Line System, or HLS.

Construction of the HLS involves the marriage of two fly lines: 1) 100 feet of a small-diameter (typically 0.029" – 0.031") floating, taperless running/shooting line, and 2) a 30-foot coil of very-fast-sinking fly line which is cut into specific lengths, ranging from 2 – 6 feet. These cut sections of sinking line are referred to as "shooting heads". Between the running line and shooting head I insert a 3-foot section of supple 30-pound monofilament, which decreases the line drag because of its smaller diameter, and allows the shooting head and flies to sink faster into the fishing zone. The interchangeable shooting heads are secured to the mono length by means of a loop-to-loop affair. Depending on the combination of current speed and depth of the water being fished, shorter or longer shooting heads are selected and looped to the running line.

In my system, here, each shooting head has a monofilament loop tied to one end, and a 4-foot leader on the other. The heads are coiled and stored in the individual clear sleeves or zip-lock plastic pocket of a leader wallet. With an indelible felt-tip marker I write on each sleeve or pocket the length of the coiled shooting head and leader it contains.

Two Nymphing Techniques on One HLS Cast

Steelhead are individuals. I must keep this in mind when I fish a steelhead run with a particular fly fished with a particular technique. I specialize in catching steelhead with the dead-drift method, utilizing a floating fly line and strike indicator. However, there are some willing-to-bite steelhead resting unseen in the water I am covering which will ignore my chosen natural drift nymph. If I employ a different presentation and maybe a different nymph or egg pattern I may induce this individual fish to bite. I learned this on those occasions I carried two strung rods ready to cast; one with floating line and indicator, the other with my Hybrid Line.

I have a favorite winter steelhead spot on the North Fork of the Alsea River. I never need a cast longer than fifty feet to cover every square inch of it. If there is a steelhead sitting in this run, it will see my fly at some point. Most days I carry the two nymphing rods just mentioned. I start methodically covering the run with the Hybrid Line set-up first.

Casting the Hybrid Line System is a matter of slinging or pitching the heavy shooting head, not using a standard back cast/forward cast, or roll cast. With good timing, the head, while flying to its target, pulls the loose coils of running line with it. It's great for casting under low-hanging tree limbs.

The HLS cast is angled upstream at 45 – 60 degrees from straight across the current. I am fishing two flies, of course, about 20 inches apart. Wintertime or early spring I pair up two egg patterns, or an egg with an egg derivative like my Hot Bead Assassin. As the flies sink and drift towards me, I gather some of the slack line, but not all of it. Basically, I am fishing the flies dead-drift, using the brightly colored running line as my strike indicator. If the drift of the line hesitates or is drawn underwater I set the hook.

Just before my flies pass my position I mend the line to continue the natural drift of the flies along the bottom. At about 45 degrees downstream I mend again to straighten the system, and allow the flies to slowly swing across the current on a tight line. Once the line has swung straight below me I allow it to hang for a few seconds on the chance a following fish will finally catch up with it to grab one of the flies.

The time is drawing close in the battle for Josh Cuperus to slide the steelhead onto the beach.

Even if I am lucky enough to catch a fish or two I am not deterred from fishing again with a floating line and strike-indicator rod. It is not unusual to hook another steelhead, one which was unwilling to fall for the HLS presentation. Conversely, on those occasions when I start with the indicator rod first I may not catch a fish, but I could entice one (or another) when I fish through the run a second time with the Hybrid Line set-up.

Fly Choices by Season

For me, steelhead fly choices vary by season. Broadly, the three general seasons for my fishing are the late-spring/summer, fall, and late-winter/early spring seasons.

For steelhead of late spring, summer, and fall I focus on flies which approximate the appearance of insects found in the rocks and rubble of the river bottom.

Stoneflies are a food staple for steelhead in Western rivers. Carry a variety of styles, sizes, and weights.

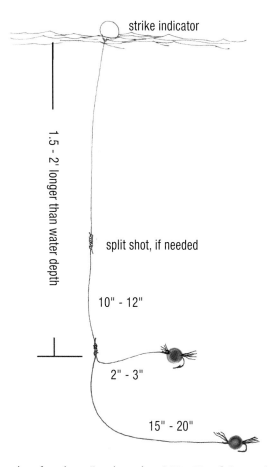

strike indicator

1.5 - 2' longer than water depth

split shot, if needed

10" - 12"

2" - 3"

15" - 20"

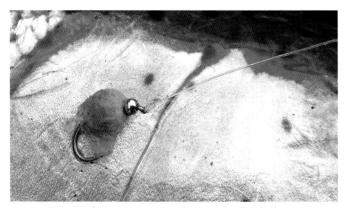

Once salmon spawning begins in the fall, egg patterns like my All-Star Bead Head Egg are top producers fall, winter, and spring.

Stonefly patterns with fluttering rubber legs and tails have special appeal to summer steelhead. The Prince, Flashback Hare's Ear, Pheasant Tail (including a few variations), and Copper John are very good choices to pair with a stonefly nymph.

During the fall, with spawning Chinook salmon in steelhead rivers, I add egg flies to my fly line up. Steelhead love salmon eggs, so I pair my Gorman Bead Egg, Sparkle Egg, or Bling Egg with the nymph pattern *du jour*. The water temperatures of the fall season here in the Pacific Northwest are warm enough to keep aquatic insects active, and the steelhead looking for them. When examining the stomach contents of hatchery fall fish it is not unusual to find a mix of insects and salmon eggs.

For winter steelhead — December through mid April — my fly pattern choices for steelhead have been reduced to a relatively small number. Whether I use a floating line and indicator or my Hybrid Line System, I use salmon egg, or egg-like patterns, the vast majority of the time. In addition to my stable of egg patterns, such as my Bead Head Egg, Sparkle Egg, Bling Egg, and Lead Eye Sparkle Egg, I use my Hot Bead Assassin in pink, orange, and chartreuse.

I prefer the small egg flies, especially when the water is low and clear. A pair of different color egg patterns work well. If the water is off-color when winter

rains raise the river, I pair a size-6 Hot Bead Assassin with an egg. It has a bigger silhouette and a flashy hot orange bead at the head, making it easier for a steelhead to locate.

Leader Set-Up Review

For nymph fishing I prefer to construct my own leaders, with quick sinkability and minimal current "push" on it, which speeds the drift of the flies. The butt section of the leader is significantly smaller than that of a standard tapered leader. For the tippet I use fluorocarbon because of its enhanced "invisibility" to the fish. The tippet will typically range in diameter from 3X to 0X (0.008" – 0.011"), depending on the sizes of the flies to be used and water clarity. In terms of breaking strength for the brands I prefer, this is 8 – 15 pounds.

In the vast majority of situations, lead wire or lead shot is employed in the system to get the flies to the depths in moving, sometimes swift, water. The weight may be incorporated into or onto the fly as it is tied. Lead wire wrapped on the hook before the fly is tied is one possibility. Lead dumbbell eyes, or a heavy bead, placed at the head of the hook as the fly is tied is an additional weight-adding procedure.

Each piece of water has its unique combination of current velocity and depth. In lieu of adding or removing split shot I will change the size of a dependable producing fly. In the summer stoneflies are a staple for a steelhead in the mood to feed. If I need more or less weight I change the size (and amount of weight in or on the fly) of the same stonefly nymph I've been fishing, or at least a proven stonefly nymph that is somewhat similar which has the desired amount of weight in it.

If the angling regulations allow, lead shot can be pinched onto the leader. I use the removable type in sizes BB and 3/0. It is important to match the amount of weight to the combination of current velocity and depth being fished. Too much weight, the flies are always dragging or stuck on the stream bottom. Too little weight, the flies drift over the heads of the fish.

Fly Position

With rare exception, I always fish multiple flies on the leader. As individuals, fish may prefer one fly to another, so I give them a choice. Additionally, since many steelhead will strike a fly only if it comes within a few inches of them I like my increased odds with the second. If one fly does not pass close enough to the steelhead to interest it, the other fly may.

This dropper set-up is the best for proper drift of the nymph and maximum hook-ability. The dropper line is no more than 3 inches long.

A common question I get asks at which position on the leader I secure the heavier of my two flies. It's an excellent question with two right answers. I have experimented with the heavier fly on both the dropper and point positions over decades, a very large sampling, and caught many steelhead each way. I have not been able to discern an effective difference. To add weight to my

research I often have one of my guided clients fish with the heavy fly on the point, while the other has the same heavy fly on the dropper. If one set-up proved more effective over the other I would set-up both anglers with identical riggings. I have no recollection of ever finding the point or dropper positions significantly advantageous or disadvantageous.

Beware of Swingers

Especially with warmer water temperatures of summer and fall, steelhead may chase a nymph as they would a swinging wet fly. When I see this happen several times during my fishing day I am inclined to put the lighterweight fly on the point because it has more swimming movement to it, and rides up off the stream bottom while the heavier fly tends to hug the bottom as it drifts. In fact, there are times I will replace the point nymph with a wet fly when the fish are in a swinging mood.

When a steelhead inhales a simple, sparse-bodied size-12 trout nymph just as if it was a meticulously tied, elaborate Intruder wet fly, it forces me to ponder how important — at times — the fly pattern is compared to the determined aggression of a particular individual steelhead. This fish may be willing to attack anything that invades its personal space. Often, it seems, the chief determining factor in eliciting a striking response from a certain steelhead is the attitude of that fish. The moral here: don't be too quick to lift the nymphs from the water for the next cast, wait until they have had a couple seconds to swing up and hold in the current. Often I have had a client hesitate before making their next cast, as I give them instructions or reminders. Sometimes lightning strikes as the nymphs hang high in the current. It is doubly important that there are no fingers pinching the fly line against the cork grip, as many anglers are wont to do. A hook-setting over-reaction at the surprise strike is a guaranteed break-off for those who insist on holding the line.

Detecting the Strike

Underwater observations and sight-fishing to visible steelhead have shown me that steelhead may hold a fly for a mere second or less before they expel it. An artificial fly does not have the texture, taste and smell of a real food item, so a fish tends to spit it out quickly. It is imperative to detect the strike immediately, and then react quickly to set the hook.

I cannot depend on feeling the strike as the steelhead takes the fly on a slack line. By the time the line would be tightened to that degree, the fish has made

One last camera pose for the steelhead before releasing it back into the depths.

its exit. However, there may be a visual indication of the strike to alert the angler to set the hook. Some will watch the tip of the floating fly line. If the line, which has some degree of slack in it to keep the flies drifting near the bottom, hesitates, stops, or is pulled under the surface, the rod tip is immediately raised to drive the hook point home. A brightly colored line is a great aid. All my floating lines are yellow, orange, fluorescent red or pale green. But a brightly colored fly line is not enough for me and my clients. It is much easier to detect a strike if I have a specific small focal point, specifically a buoyant hi-vis strike indicator. This is attached to the upper portion of my leader, anywhere from two inches to two feet from the fly line. For me, the ideal distance from the indicator to the dropper fly is 1 1/2 to 2 feet longer than the water depth. While riding the current, if the indicator deviates in any way from its natural drift I set the hook. Downstream and across.

I try to emphasize to nymphers how subtle the strike from a large fish can be. With occasional exceptions, steelhead do not aggressively attack a drifting nymph. They casually move over and intercept it. Especially in slower currents, the indicator will barely hesitate when taken by a fish, and then it will immediately release it

so the flies and indicator continue on their downstream journey. Because a gentle take and release can be easily overlooked for the beginner or the unaware, I plead with my anglers to seek any reason to set the hook. *Any* reason.

I watch indicator drifts all day on a typical steelhead day, virtually every single cast made by both anglers in my boat. If I haven't seen a million indicator drifts in my career I'll wager I'm getting close. If, out of the blue, I suggest to someone that he or she should set the hook they need to trust me. When I hear in reply "That couldn't have been a fish" or "I think that was a rock", I ask the angler to humor me and to please participate in my eccentric experiment to set the hook. I wish I had a dollar for every time I have heard, "I can't believe it! It really WAS a fish."

Certain pieces of water I fish are relatively snag free, the bottom being very nymphing friendly. In such waters if the indicator does something out of the ordinary I know it's a fish. When I suggest, "Set the Hook!" my guest may maintain "It was a rock." So, I hold the boat in the same position we were located in when the "rock" grabbed the fly, and gently ask the angler to hit the rock again with their nymphs. It's interesting how the flies cannot find the rock a second time, even after two dozen casts. Sometimes they do find the rock again . . . cleverly disguised as a steelhead. Then, all in attendance enjoy a laughing Holy S#!&! moment.

Location, Location, Location

The correct indicator position on the leader is important. Ideally, I prefer to locate my indicator so that the distance between it and my uppermost (dropper) fly is 1 1/2 – 2 feet greater than the water depth. Since the water depth varies from one fishing location to the next I will change the distance often. Too much distance between flies and indicator, and the delay between the interception of the fly by a fish and the hesitation or sinking of the indicator is increased. Too short a distance, the flies may float over the head of a fish that may strike a fly if it was at eye level or drifting along the stream bottom.

It's tragic when the *upper* portion of the leader breaks during the battle with a big steelhead on the hook. Because the metal grommet on popular soft-plastic bubble indicators can eventually fray the leader I often locate multiple snap swivels along the upper portion of the leader. The swivels make for a secure connection and a quick change of the indicator.

Using a swivel on the leader prevents line wear that can lead to a break-off.

Put on the brakes, exit the boat, and make the scoop. Chaaa-ching.

It's Game Day!

My preparation has been completed the night before my fishing or guiding day. Rods are already strung and ready to fish when I hit the river as I seek to maximize fishing time. If I am with clients, they aren't paying me to take a chunk out of their fishing day assembling rods, stringing fly lines, and tying on flies. My guests are paying me to enable them to catch steelhead. In this competitive environment, I want to be focused on immediately getting into position to fish the likely water thoroughly and quickly. Then, it's time to get to the next piece of water, and the next, and the next. On-the-river equipment prep is wasted time if it is something I could have accomplished the previous night. Preparation is a building block of a successful game plan.

The day will naturally produce delays and situations that will detract from fishing time, such as line tangles, fly break-offs, and wilderness bathroom breaks. Whether fishing for myself or with clients I am trying to think three moves ahead on the angling chessboard. I'm factoring time, the quality "rating" of water to be fished (or to be left un-fished), particular challenges with any given piece of water, such as overhanging trees, snaggy zones, the ability to hold on anchor (or not), other anglers, and the skill sets of my clients. More than 35 years in pursuit of steelhead has taught me many lessons about how to maximize effective fishing time, and I use them every day I am on the water.

From an elevated position, currents and likely holding water can be studied carefully. With a high sun and binoculars fish can often be sighted.

Focusing on Productive Water

As the fishing day begins I'm thinking of the first spot I'm hoping I, or my clients, will fish. I am very particular since my we cannot catch fish where they are not. I'm seeking current flows that approximate a "walking pace" with *unidirectional* currents. There may be exceptions, but I start my search with a common-sense estimation. If the surface waters are choppy or riffly, so much the better, since this feature will distort the fishes' vision as I approach.

For effective presentation of the nymph, especially with guests, I seek out water I estimate to be three to seven feet deep, just over my head at the extreme depth. Even though steelhead may hold in shallower or deeper water than this suggested range, three to seven feet maximizes my chances, and my clients', when I factor in stealth, line control, and detection of a subtle strike. After stating this, there are certain situations where I will lengthen my leader to fish water up to ten feet deep to challenge myself. I know that if another fly-angler has fished this water before my arrival I may have a chance to get my nymphs in front of a fish that has not seen flies today. Also, steelhead hanging near the bottom in deep water are not as easily disturbed by other anglers and boaters, and thus, may be in the mood to bite if I can get my flies in front of them.

The third consideration to enhance locating a likely hot target is underwater structure. Boulders, ledges, scooped depressions, and transitions from shallow water to deep are all appealing resting areas for steelhead. Swirling eddies immediately behind exposed midstream boulders intrigue the inexperienced angler. I want unidirectional, not swirling, multidirectional currents. Depending on its shape and surrounding depth, exposed boulders may have steelhead holding in front or on either side of them. Fully submerged boulders do not present this eddying problem to the same degree.

Preferred steelhead lies change as the river flow increases or decreases. Yesterday's hotspot may no longer hold fish as the water drops or rises. At any water level, I search out those locations that fit the three general parameters I have just suggested.

Is it an alien sucking the brains from a steelhead, or is it Tome Gerding with a kiss good-bye?

Good rainbow trout holding water is steelhead holding water. Those readers who can recognize good rainbow fishing water, can easily transition to locating prime steelhead water. The only two water types that I will fish for trout but ignore for steelhead are eddies and cut banks. Steelhead may hold in eddies but they are extremely hard to nymph effectively. Because steelhead are migratory, on-the-move creatures, they would not hang out very long in a cut-bank area, if at all.

Today's Flies

After many years of nymphing a broad array of steelhead rivers I have a good feel for the flies to be fished on my familiar waters. Seasonality and river conditions have a bearing on my choices.

In western North America many of our inland (non-coastal) rivers are insect-rich. I's only natural that migrating steelhead, hungry or not, will encounter daily aquatic insects drifting, swimming, or emerging in the water column. If a steelhead should be in a snacking mood food is at hand. One commonly available insect group is stonefly nymphs. The larger species may have a three-year life cycle, so they are omnipresent. Stonefly nymph imitations are in my stable of go-to flies. Because some of the insects can exceed two inches in length, in addition to the smaller-size generations in the river at the same time, I may have the exact same stonefly patterns tied in four different sizes, each having a progressive amount of physical weight. By switching out one fly size for another I can have the ideal amount of weight on my leader for any given piece of water. This is particularly important in fly-fishing-only waters where no external weights may be attached to the leader. Besides catching fish, my stonefly serves as a legal weight to get the smaller second fly to the river bottom.

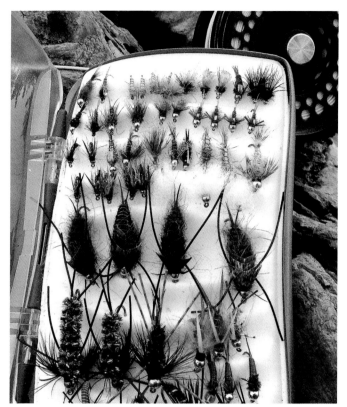

A contrast in sizes, my steelhead nymphs range in size from 4 to 14.

Paired with the stonefly nymph summer through early fall I usually select a fly that approximates the sizes of smaller insect fare in the river, usually mayflies and caddisflies. Though it may sound a little crazy to fish a size-12 or -14 "trout" fly for a steelhead which can exceed 10 pounds, there are some days every fish put in the net has opted for the small fly in my two-fly set-up.

While fishing the Rogue River for steelhead Eric Gorman found a fall chinook salmon on the end of his line instead.

It is not unusual to catch migrating fall Chinook salmon on nymphs when casting for steelhead, including little size-12 Prince Nymphs, Copper Johns, or Flashback Hare's Ears. Some of these fish will top 20 pounds! On a trout nymph. During the 2014 summer steelhead season my clients landed 15 *fair-hooked* Chinook salmon on nymphs. A spicy bonus to a fishing day.

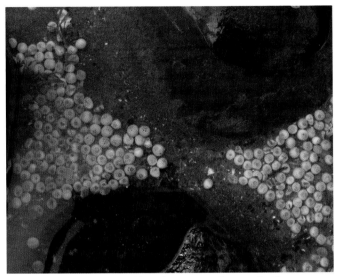

Salmon and steelhead eggs can be washed out of their nests, providing tempting snacks for steelhead fall, winter, and spring.

When the fall Chinook start spawning in mid September, one of my egg patterns — my Bead Egg, Sparkle Egg, or Bling Egg — will be paired with the stonefly nymph. If the fish are hard after eggs only, I will tie on a weighted Dumbbell-Eye Sparkle Egg which will act to get both flies to the bottom. Since I carry this pattern in three sizes I can switch these flies to get the right amount of weight to match any piece of water I am

When fishing a pair of egg flies I prefer to have one of the two weighted with dumbbell eyes.

fishing. Fishing two eggs allows me to experiment with color, size, and pattern. Winter and early spring — fishing for winter steelhead — I am fishing two egg flies, or an egg paired with a Hot Bead Assassin.

Add a Little Life

To enhance the swimming fishability of my flies, especially the smaller ones, sometimes I will secure the nymph to the leader with a Duncan loop. This slip knot, which I can open and close to the size I want, allows the nymph to wiggle and swim, enhancing the illusion it is alive and tasty dining fare. A size-14 fly is best suited to being fished convincingly on a 5X (0.006" diameter) tippet. So when I tie this to a 2X (0.009") steelhead tippet it does not have much lively movement as it drifts towards a potentially-interested fish. When using a Duncan loop I prefer to use it for the point fly. If I use it on the dropper fly, and I wish to change it out for another pattern, I must reconstruct that portion of the leader since there may not be enough line length to tie on another fly.

A slip knot like the Duncan loop can create a bit of life-like movement in the nymph to entice a steelhead to bite.

Upstream or Downstream Nymphing Position

If I am on foot, wading into a likely looking run, I prefer to position myself at the downstream end of the run I have chosen to fish. Since fish face into the current, I am approaching them from behind. With quiet wading, I can get relatively close to a steelhead's position without alarming it. When fishing from a boat, I start at the upstream end of the run and fish it downstream. Because the fish are facing me, and I have a much higher profile standing in the boat I cannot get as close to the fish as I can while wading.

Since most of the time I am unable to locate the fish visually, I must methodically cover the likely holding water.

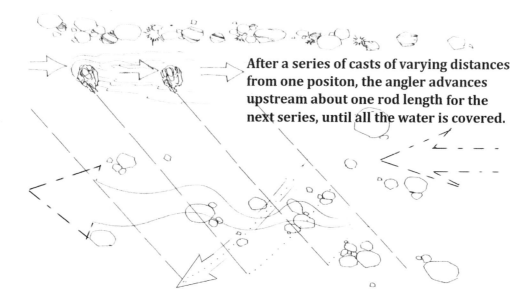

After a series of casts of varying distances from one positon, the angler advances upstream about one rod length for the next series, until all the water is covered.

Assuming I can wade close to the water I am fishing, my first cast may land the flies no more than two rod lengths. The cast is angled upstream at 45 to 60 degrees from straight across the current. As the flies drift back with the current toward me, they should quickly sink. To that end, I gather some of the slack by merely raising my rod tip on a short cast, but not all of the slack, leaving about two feet of the floating fly line on the water. In so doing I have an excellent balance between too much slack and too little. A few seconds after the flies hit the water I mend the fly line. Once the line and flies have passed my position on their journey downstream I begin to lower my rod tip slowly to give back line, maintaining a little slack until the current finally pulls the whole system tight at the end of the drift.

Effective nymphing is a short-line game, usually played out within thirty-five feet. From my initial position I make a dozen good casts of varying lengths, then move up- or downstream by about a rod length and start my casting routine again. On foot I prefer to cover the water from the lower end of the run progressing upstream, so I am approaching the fish from behind as they face into the current. A typical first cast is no more than a rod-length of fly line. I repeat the cast but change the angle slightly. For the next two casts I lengthen the line a couple of feet. Make two casts, and then lengthen until I have reached my maximum effective fishing distance, or completely covered the good fishing water. I'm thorough, and make sure not to ignore the short casts. Sometimes a steelhead will hold in the water underneath my rod tip. I have seen it happen many times, and

if the angler ignores some of the prime water closest to him, a willing biter may have been bypassed.

On the days I am guiding, virtually all fishing is done from my drift boat. From a higher vantage point casting and mending are more easily accomplished. When using two-hand rods measuring 13 feet or more, even rookies can cast and mend well in a short time when following my simple directions.

Effective Mending Quick Review

Proper mending and the correct direction of the hook-set are the two most critical steelhead fishing skills I teach on the river. However, for those who don't mend properly, they may not have to be concerned whatsoever with setting the hook. Experienced "experts" are my most difficult students. Muscle memory habits of a lifetime are hard to reprogram.

Without adjustment, a fly line fished across the current, either floating or drifting in the upper portion of the water column, will eventually race ahead of the nymphs as they sink toward the bottom where the current velocity is much slower. When steelhead prefer a slow natural drift of the flies, those nymphs moving at an unnatural speed will be ignored.

Effectively mending the fly line is crucial to slowing the drift of the fly, minimizing drag, and preventing the flies from coursing too quickly. Mending can be the difference between fishing success and failure. It's that important! Not all mends are created equal. It is so common for me to see anglers attempt to mend with the rod tip waist high. The rod tip should be positioned *high*

Think: Turn the jump rope. Good mends can make the difference in enticing (or not enticing) a reluctant steelhead to bite.

(eye-high or higher) to flip/reposition the slack in the fly line upstream of the nymph. Multiple mends may be necessary during a single drift.

I find the most effective, long-lasting mend is one where I position three to eight of fly line directly upstream of my indicator, in the same current line as the indicator. This removes the pulling influence of the fly line and leader on the flies.

Turn the jump rope. Higher. That's it.

With a little push during the mend, several feet of fly line will be positioned directly upstream in the same current line as the leader and indicator, allowing for an excellent dead-drift of the flies.

Hit and Run

The first time a willing steelhead, a player, sees a convincing drift of the nymphs near its holding position it is most likely to strike one or the other. For this reason once my guests or I have systematically and completely covered a piece of water it's time to move to the next. To accomplish the thorough covering of the run we are fishing I am watching each drift of the flies, offering directions and encouragement until the mission is accomplished.

If someone hooks a fish a natural question is whether or not other steelhead in the vicinity are disturbed to the point they will not bite. It's been my experience that at least some of the fish are not put off. In fact, some may be "awakened" out of their lethargy and, then, be willing to bite. It is not unusual to sometimes catch a second, third, or fourth steelhead out of the same general location.

During my high season I may be on the river for ten consecutive days or more. My longest streak of consecutive steelheading days is 28. I may fish the same section of river for multiple consecutive days so I have a good sense of exactly where the fish are. A particular location, such as The Fish Hotel or Magic Rock, may produce fish (sometimes multiple fish) for two or three days in a row, and then no fish for a day or two. Steelhead are migratory nomads, so I cannot depend on catching fish every day at each good fishing spot I have, even my very best locations. And, there's a very good chance someone else may have fished my chosen spot before I did, catching or at least disturbing any fish that I or my guests might have hooked. So, I must discover many possible

If you want an audience while fighting a steelhead, hook one as you drift through town. It's Chuck Beck with the rod and guide Jeff Elston on the oars.

My young guest Raji Maki poses with his very first steelhead. What a special event for both of us!

fish-holding locations on a river for my own angling efforts or those of my clients so there is always one more place to fish. I can't be the infamous One Trick Pony with only one or two proven fishing spots.

My ideal section of river, whether I'm on foot or in my boat, will have twenty or more reliable fishing spots. Some days when the fishing is exceptional I will only need ten or twelve specific locations to fill an eight-hour fishing day. Other days, two dozen spots are barely enough, especially when there are many anglers on the river competing for the same locations. Part of my daily strategic game plan involves assessing the degree of competition with which I will have to contend. If I know the competition is high I may add some of my secondary locations to the itinerary in addition to my best ones which may be open to fish. I know that some of the water I would hope to fish will be occupied. I will make critical judgments during a high-traffic day about where to fish and how long to linger in any given fishing spot.

Fishing my secondary locations will sometimes produce a steelhead or two, and perhaps these spots can salvage a tough fishing day. In fact, it's possible that a secondary spot may evolve into a first-tier location. Each year rivers change, either because of high wintertime flows or the occasional flood event. Some of my all-time favorite fishing spots have been permanently altered by high water, never to fish well again. At the same time, a secondary piece of water may be beneficially changed to fish well. Also, floods may create brand-new holding-water zones where none existed before. More puzzle solving to be done. It is my job to discover the new, and, perhaps, bypass formerly dependable areas which no longer attract steelhead to linger on their journeys.

Dr. Gorman Will See You Now

On those fishing days when steelhead are caught — sometimes four or five, or ten! — as the poet Robert Browning said " . . . God's in his heaven — All's right with the world!" I am naturally upbeat. My fishing companions are cheery and talkative, recounting the day's successes and bloopers. What fun.

And then there are those inevitable days when nothing seems to go quite right on the river. My backlog of experience and understanding of steelhead help me deal with a day when no fish were brought to hand. I know that tough days make the successful ones that much sweeter. However, not all my guests, clients, and fishing companions can cope with the challenges steelhead lay before them. If it's day one of a two- or three-day fishing event, there's a, "We'll get 'em tomorrow" encouragement

Tiny fish grow to be big fish. Joann Severson finds humor in catching a small fry (pun intended) on heavy-duty steelhead gear and a nymph that appears too big to swallow.

Who is this masked man? Might be steelhead nymphing ace Mark Severson. Maybe.

coming from me, and it seems to always lift everyone's hopes, especially if I start laying out tomorrow's game plan of where we will go and what we will do differently. And I sincerely believe we will, indeed, catch fish, or more fish, tomorrow.

If my clients and companions are fishing with me for only one day, there is no tomorrow. So if fish-catching expectations are not met, Dr. Gorman must console and encourage. I recount what they may have learned, the pleasant weather, the beautiful day, the deer and wild turkeys we saw, and an analysis of why we did not land as many steelhead as hoped. Fortunately for me, at this stage in my career a skunk day is rare. However, some anglers believe that since I am a professional steelhead guide, teacher, and author that steelhead go suicidal when I show up. I wish it were so.

Change Can Be Good

Inertia, as I talked about before, is resistance to change until acted upon by a force. One of the forces in a fishing day which causes me to act, to change, is not being able to find biting steelhead. There are certain spots I fish on every river I know well that I know hold fish today, the day I'm fishing it. It is such locations I will fish thoroughly with the method and flies I have fished up to this point in the day. Then, I'm going to fish it again. I will either change the flies, or I will change the presentation, or I may change both. In summertime, I will switch to a

This unnamed experimental nymph caught a beautiful summer steelhead for its creator Mark Severson on its maiden voyage. Of course it has now won a place in his fly box.

completely different stonefly pattern and I will change out the size, color or pattern of the smaller fly. If I am fishing with two guests I will have each of them use different flies, so I will be experimenting with four nymphs instead of two. In late fall and winter, I will change up the egg fly or Hot Bead Assassin sizes, colors, and pattern style. As for presentation, I may switch to presenting the flies with my Hybrid Line System instead of the floating line and indicator set-up. At the next place we fish where I know fish are definitely holding, I may very well change flies and methods again. Or, I may change the section of river I fish tomorrow. If I'm still at a loss for an immediate answer, the best choice may be to move to a different river. Options are vital.

Time to Cowboy Up!

Those days when it seems that there is not a biting fish in the river are my best opportunities to learn something as I sort through the puzzle, change flies and methods, experiment, think about what I would do differently next time. It could be that the steelhead refused to bite today, and there was really nothing that could be done to change their little minds. Even if this is true, if I accept that possibility, I will stop trying to find the answer, to ponder, to experiment, to excel. This is a Challenger level steelhead Sudoku puzzle. I embrace it. There IS an answer, and I will find it.